Identity Cry-Sis

Cassandra Karch

Identity Cry-Sis
Copyright © 2022 Cassandra Karch

ISBN: 979-8-9862438-0-1

Edited by: Cate Perry
Design: Parker Graphics

DEDICATION

To my amazing children,

I LOVE YOU WITH ALL OF ME!!

CONTENTS

"I'm not saying I'm gonna change the world, but I guarantee that I will spark the brain that will change the world."[1]

Tupac Amaru Shakur

"Always do your best, don't let the pressure make you panic."

Tupac Amaru Shakur

Please follow for upcoming book events

Instagram @identitycry_sis

INTRODUCTION

The Hate You Give Little Infants Fucks Everyone (T.H.U.G.L.I.F.E.)[2], but what about the hate I gave myself. You've seen it, I've experienced it; now let's go back to how we got here. I'm ready to share my story with the world. This journey has taken me 45 laps around the sun, but because of God, the marathon continues. These are my truths; taken from my memory and stories I've heard. Some may be a little jaded, and people's names have been changed to protect other's identities, but I hope you find comfort within its pages. Some of you may be experiencing or have experienced similar challenges in your lives. I want you to know you are not alone. While I began writing this story in 2014, it wasn't until early 2021 that I was led to finish it. As you ride this wave with me, you'll get to know me and all of my craziness and you'll see the world through my eyes. It has been my experience that when you don't know yourself, you will listen to any other voice to figure out who you are or you will give into the emotions of whom you think you should be. This was me.

Can I tell you a secret? No one else in this world has your fingerprints. You are God's masterpiece! And so am I! I thank God

---

2

for creating me and you in his image and likeness. He fashioned the finest jewelry when He formed us! **THERE IS NO ONE ELSE LIKE YOU!** I believe it, do you?

I'm grateful for God's protection through all the trials I've experienced in my life! HALLELUJAH! I don't look like what I've been through! My prayer for you is that, after reading this book, you will be in touch with your "true self", the one God intends for you to be.

David tells us in Psalm 139:14 that he praises God because He made us in such a wonderful way. How amazing is that? Even down to the hairs on the tops of our heads, God knew what He was doing when he formed you and me. Our bodies, our minds, and our spirits are the work of God. All of us have a journey worth traveling; never stop exploring yours.

Today, I challenge you to walk according to your divine purpose and know that you are designed for such a time as this.

CHAPTER 1
IDENTITY CRY-SIS

How would you maneuver through life if you felt you didn't belong? Would you try to fit in? Would you try to disappear? Or would you act like a chameleon and change colors to blend in with your surroundings? Now, imagine being a child of color born into a family with whom some are racists. Like a Catch-22. You feel as if your white family didn't accept you and your Black family didn't want you.

Growing up, I had a conflicted view of myself. I am Black but I am also white and sometimes get caught between the two. People always said that I needed to pick a side. Why?

The story of my life was as follows: I felt all alone in the world, never belonging to anything or anyone, and trying to find my place. Over time, it got harder because I didn't have anybody I could confide in and the things I saw and heard, day in and day out, confused me. People would say to me, "You were born with that good hair!" But what makes my hair good, when I had no idea what to do with it? Even now, I hear *my* people say, "She thinks she's better than you because of her light skin." What the hell does my light skin have to do with who I am? If I cut you and you cut me, we will both bleed red, point blank, period!

These constant micro-aggressions led me to make decisions that didn't benefit me, all because I was trying to fit in others people's little boxes. The desire to belong to something or someone was strong in me. What was my identity? Who was I? It's very hard to know who you are when you don't know where you come from. In my opinion, a lot of us black and brown folks have this problem, especially those of mixed ethnicities.

As you continue through the pages of this book, I hope you will understand a little better why these questions came up for me.

I shed a lot of tears by operating in fear and now my faith is guiding me through the next 45 years. Thank You, JESUS!

Identity is defined by the Webster dictionary: who someone is: the name of a person: the qualities, beliefs, etc., which makes a particular person or group different from others
Cry: shed tears, typically as an expression of distress, pain, or sorrow
Sis: a person's sister (often used as a form of address). My definition of a sis, in this aspect, is a sista: a black woman!

CHAPTER 2
SODA CAN MIRACLE

As a child, I was told that when my mom was pregnant with me, my great-grandmother ordered her to get an abortion because she didn't want any 'nigger' children in her family. Although I never heard her say anything mean to me, I rarely saw her either. My great-grandmother was conditioned to believe she was better than those who didn't look like her, and that; prejudice extended to black and brown people. During my grandma Soper's childhood, she often went to play at the "colored kid's" house, but her mother would refuse to let "those people" into their home. It wasn't until I turned 18 that my great-grandmother stopped thinking of me as "those people" and accepted me as family.

My mom was a very smart girl. A straight-A student, destined for greatness, she was supposed to go off and study abroad in Europe. But then the unimaginable happened. At the age of thirteen she was on her way to school standing at a bus stop on Rainer Ave and Graham Street in South Seattle when she was grabbed by a man. That man dragged her to a nearby apartment and raped her. To this day, I don't believe the man was ever caught or brought to justice. That event changed my mom from that day forward. As a result, she lost confidence in herself, her abilities, and ultimately her dream to study abroad. It is even possible that she blamed herself for what happened, as many victims do.

When my mom was fourteen, she first met my dad and he instantly swept her off her feet with his "charm". He made it his business to make her feel special and loved. In his words, she was the most beautiful girl he had ever seen. Thus, began the love affair between my white mother and my Black father.

My dad claims he was a nerd before he met my mom, but I find that hard to believe. Everything she did revolved around him and he was always her focus. As young teenagers, they believed they loved each other but the world wasn't accepting of their love. Society didn't want to see dating between different races. Although the state of Washington was more open-minded and lifted the interracial marriage ban in 1868, my parents still felt the sting of racism. In some of the places they traveled together, my mom was called a "nigger lover." It wasn't until 1967 when the Supreme Court decided in, *Loving Vs Virginia*, that all state interracial laws were unconstitutional. I was born in 1975, so that law was still relatively new. My dad was fifteen years old the first time he was stopped by white police officers and choked out to almost death, just for walking while Black in the neighborhood. As he struggled for air in the back of the police car, the officer in the front seat saw someone walking toward the vehicle and motioned for him to stop. That someone was his mother, my Grandma Jeanette.

She walked up to the car and asked, "What is going on here?"

The officer politely responded, "Oh nothing, we were just having a conversation."

My dad got out of the car, straightened his shirt, and quietly walked down the street with his mom. He never did tell Grandma Jeanette what happened. Can you imagine the type of fear and trauma he experienced at that moment? The same fears persist today, as Black and brown people are still targeted by some police officers based on the color of their skin.

At the age of sixteen, my parents found themselves in a very different situation. Suddenly, my mom was pregnant. As a teenager and expecting, she had to shift gears. Although she thought she had until November to prepare for my arrival, a car accident resulted in my premature birth. In fact, I was born three months early. As a result of being 13 weeks early, my eyes were still fused shut, and my lungs were underdeveloped, so I struggled to take a breath. My doctors told my mom I wouldn't make it, but God had other plans for me (*insert praise dance here*). At birth, I weighed 2 pounds 11 ounces, and measured 5 inches long. I was held by my grandpa Don in the palm of his hand. Imagine that a standard soda can is 4.83 inches high and 2.6 inches wide. Do you see it? That was me.

I then started to lose weight and I dropped down to 1 pound 15 ounces. For months, I was kept in an incubator while my organs developed. My mom would have to wait a while to hold me in her arms, and the nurses weren't very encouraging either. After 5 long months, I was strong enough to go home. The doctors said one thing, but God had the final say. Look at me now! The fight in me when I was an infant and the fight in me now, I give all praises to God and my ancestors. I am truly a miracle! God had a plan for my life way back then! And He has a plan for yours.

Please do me a favor. Never quit fighting for your life! Fight for your happiness, fight for your peace, and fight for your health! **FIGHT FOR EVERYTHING!** We should be living our *heaven* here on earth, but we must fight for it!

CHAPTER 3
RAINIER VISTA

When I was a baby, my family lived in a neighborhood called Yesler Terrace, the very first public housing in downtown Seattle. Apparently, these complexes were the first racially integrated public housing development in the United States at that time.[3] It was a one-bedroom apartment for the three of us. When we lived there, my dad worked two jobs to keep us afloat, but that didn't last long. My parents didn't get along and my dad would overstep his boundaries with my mom, sometimes putting his hands on her. He was a young teenage father who probably hadn't even experienced puberty yet. He knew he needed to mature, so he left. Once he was gone, my mom found out she was pregnant again.

When I was 3 ½ years old, my mom moved my new baby sister and me to Rainier Vista; not the new development that now stands, but the old one with the single-level duplexes. We lived near Martin Luther King Jr Way and South Alaska Street. During that time, it was a very dangerous place to live. Our home would get broken into quite often, and I never could understand why? What made our house a target? My dad wasn't living with us and people in the neighborhood knew it. He parented us from a distance, and for

_____

[3]

most of our childhood, he was either in the streets hustling, or he was serving time in prison.

As it turned out, people still couldn't accept the fact that my mom, a white woman, could have Black kids. Home invasions were frequent at our residence. During one of those many break-ins, our house was vandalized. Someone cut the eye out of a velvet portrait we had on the wall, taped the eye on a piece of paper, and wrote the words, "We are watching you." The piece of paper was taped to the refrigerator and left there for us to see. There wasn't anything my mom could do to secure our house and we always felt uneasy. Our home was supposed to be our safe space but it always seemed as if we were in harm's way. I couldn't understand why.

When another break-in occurred at our house, my sister saw a hole in the window and she wanted to play. She stuck her head through the broken glass and began to jump up and down, cutting the top of her head straight across. Now at that time, we were really poor and we didn't own a phone. My mom was on her way to the neighbor's house to call 911 when two Black ladies blindsided her and beat her up. They believed she was having an affair with one of their boyfriends. The scene remains vivid in my memory: in front of the entire neighborhood, two Black women beat her up: one bald-headed dark skinned woman and a light-skinned woman with an afro. There seemed to be every neighbor present in a giant circle around the grass area near our house, watching as these two Black ladies beat the crap out of my mom, swinging her around by her beautiful black hair. They punched her in the face, most likely breaking her nose.

As I watched my mom suffer, I cried and screamed at the window. Although I cannot recall how the beating ended, I do remember that when the police arrived, nothing happened. My mom was standing there with a bloodied towel and a black and blue face, yet these officers weren't interested in helping her. According to the police officers, all residents they interviewed in the neighborhood said nothing had happened.

As I sat there sniffling and watching my mom talk to the police I felt anger rise inside me. I said to myself, "You are the police, you are supposed to help and yet you're not helping." "What kind of people are you?" As a child, I learned that the police don't always help people like me, especially when we are poor. My mom had to take my sister to the hospital and she herself needed assistance. At times, the projects were hellholes. The prejudice and racism were out of control. Sad to say it still runs rampant today. The sight of my mom getting beaten up left a bad taste in my mouth when it came to Black people. My people! At that very moment, I began to struggle with my identity. My internal voice told me that Black people were evil.

Carefully Consider This...

You may have struggled with a part of your individuality as well. During your formative years, you may have experienced events that influenced your inner self. As you visualized the hostility our family suffered, you felt your heart beat fast. Those feelings are normal. Make sure you are not blaming yourself for what happened. Instead, channel those thoughts and emotions into something positive. Understand that those situations were out of your control. Although you couldn't prevent what happened then, you can prevent what occurs now. Let's be the change we want to see. By spreading love and not hate we can make this world a better place.

CHAPTER 4
HIGH POINT

When I was five, we moved into another project. You would think this project was better, but it was a lot of the same and sometimes worse. High Point is located in West Seattle; it looks so different in today's time, due to a Seattle Housing Authority redevelopment project that took place in 2006. Most of the streets we grew up on in that neighborhood no longer exist. Our house was right across the street from the big field near the old gym. We have many great and not-so-great memories from our old neighborhood, but in the end, we are all family!

While we lived in High Point, a lot of things happened to other kids in the hood, but my focus is on me and my siblings. We didn't have much money and didn't always have food to eat. Do you remember the powdered milk and powdered eggs we used to get back in the day? I find it fascinating that while the government thought it was helping, it was slowly poisoning us with that processed junk.

When I was seven years old, these Asian people would come around the neighborhood and offer us food. They would pick us up in their nice cars and drive us to this big house, which would have some type of Asian writing on the walls. We would all be in a room, kneeling on our knees with our faces to the ground and chanting, *"Nam Myoho Renge Kyo"*. Of course, we didn't know what those words meant, but what we did know is that we got food after we repeated that chant repeatedly for about thirty minutes to an hour. Food made us happy, especially since we didn't have a lot of food at home. I learned later in life that those particular Asians were associated with the Buddhist religion and the chant we were saying was a central mantra chanted within all forms of Nichiren Buddhism.[4] Basically, we were chanting in repentance for our sins of the past and present, trying to obtain an awakening or a balance. Repentance is necessary to move forward in life and achieve forgiveness.

As believers in God, we are taught to serve others and love unconditionally and those Asian people did just that. They treated us as one of their own. It didn't matter that we were Black and they were Asian; what mattered was that they served their purpose to help us. The Word of God teaches us that we should uplift and help others, and we too will be uplifted and helped. In my opinion, we are here on this earth to make it a better place for all humans.

We were often in need, but one person who always stood by us was my mother's mom, Grandma Soper. I developed asthma as a young child and would have asthma attacks often. I couldn't have been more than eight years old when I had my first major attack. For some reason, my mom always thought I was playing around when I wasn't. I called Grandma Soper crying and unable to breathe and she would jump in her car and drive the eight miles as quickly as she could from Burien to West Seattle to take me to the hospital. One time, she was pulled over by the police, going 55 in a 35 mph zone. She explained to the officer that her granddaughter was having an asthma attack and she needed to get to her immediately. The officer led her the whole way with his sirens and lights blazing, of course, as he wanted to make sure she was telling the truth. The officer let her

---

4

off with a warning and instructed her to call 911 the next time. On the other occasions when she had to speed to get me to the hospital, she was never pulled over, and she always got me there!

In my eyes, Grandma Soper was the best grandma ever. She would never allow us to go hungry and always made sure we had clothes and shoes to wear. She and Grandpa Soper were locksmiths, so they made good money. Every year when school started, she would take us shopping for two outfits and a new pair of shoes. Some kids can be mean if you come to school with used hand-me-down clothes, especially if some of those clothes were donated by the parents of those kids. Since we would usually get hand-me-downs from the Clothes Closet near the Girls Club of Puget Sound, it was only natural that we would wear some of the other kids' clothes. My grandma Soper knew we needed to feel confident and fit in at school, so regardless of whether that happened or not, I knew I always had a place with her.

Unfortunately, I didn't get that kind of attention from my mom. She was usually not available for us kids. She struggled with depression, covering our windows with dark sheets so that sunlight never streamed in. Craving my mom's attention and affection, I would walk my siblings down the super long hill from High Point to K-mart, and encourage my siblings to steal little things, while I stole cigarettes. At age nine, I tried to fit in with cool kids in my neighborhood when I smoked my first cigarette. I also remember a time when I was ten years old and we had just come home from K-mart. I decided to sit on the bench in my backyard by myself and smoke a cigarette. My siblings were climbing the tree in the front yard. I lit up the cigarette, took one puff and there was my mom standing there. With her right hand on her hip and her left finger-pointing, she yelled at the top of her lungs, "What the hell do you think you are doing"? I froze, my heart beating hard in my chest. There was no way I was getting out of this one. In a rage, my mom slapped me across the face, knocking the cigarette from my hand and saying "get my butt in the house." I cried and ran inside terrified of what would happen.

As I sat there on my bed ready to receive her lashing, my heart raced a thousand miles a minute. I was crying uncontrollably and mom told me to shut my mouth. As I saw her reach out with an open hand, I closed my eyes and felt the sting on my face.

I screamed, "I am sorry mom!"

But that didn't move her to stop.

She yelled, "You're not sorry, or you would quit acting up!"

She whooped me good over that nonsense. She was no joke when it came to discipline. I stripped naked, got in the tub, got soaking wet, and she tore up my ass with the telephone cord.

As a result of that beating, my butt was black and blue. It took me a few months before I picked up a cigarette again.

Some might even say I was abused as a child. But you know what the cold part about that situation was? After my mom beat me up, I would take it out on our cat. Our cat's name was Suzy Q, and I would throw that cat against the wall. After all, they have nine lives, right? The thing is that cat knew unconditional love because she always came back – just like I did with my mom.

Clearly, I was not a good role model for my siblings. I was the oldest of three but had lots to learn. Since I was trying so hard to fit in, I just did whatever everyone else did. Most of the time, we learned these games from the older teens our neighborhood. Who remembers the childhood game Hide and Go Get It? As someone who grew up in a hood like me, I see you raising your hand. You would run and hide from the boys and when you got caught, they would hump you and kiss you! What about the game, Seven Minutes in Heaven? The kids would run and disperse, and if they got caught, they had seven minutes to make out, get freaky, and possibly have sex. All of ten years old, and I thought I was grown.

I did some messed-up things and had a twisted outlook on what fun was. At one point I coerced these kids who were younger than me to play the game. We would go back to the woods near Snake Hill and play those games. Those kids told their parents what I did and the police were called. My mom almost lost custody of me and I had to undergo counseling with a social worker.

I was becoming desperate to belong but was slow to realize that copying the kids around me was like me trying to put my foot in a shoe that was one size too small. No matter how hard I tried, it just wouldn't go in. If in fact, I ever did squeeze my foot into that shoe, I inevitably ended up with corns and husks on my toes.

My mom had lots of boyfriends, and most of these men left a bad taste in my mouth. She always dated Black men. Although I think this was her way of helping us find our identity, it didn't work for me because so many of the men she chose had done bad things to her. They would hit her and force her to do favors for them. To this day, I think something happened to me. I used to have nightmares of a man breaking into our home, getting on top of me, having his way. Sadly, I've never been able to find the source of that memory. It must've been one of the many men who came through our home. Several kids in our neighborhood were molested, but no one wanted to discuss it. Black communities don't talk about sexual abuse. The saying goes, what happens in the house stays in the house. The experience must be dealt with privately, by remaining silent. It would bring our families embarrassment if we spoke up. When we do tell someone, we are not believed and are forced to relive the trauma again. So we keep our mouths shut.

At one point, my mom had a boyfriend named Lonnie. He was Black. Lonnie was a nice guy, but he did some stupid things. He used to put dishwashing soap in the orange soda to see which one of us was drinking it. It turned out it was my mom who got sick from ingesting the poison.

He also had entanglements with other women in the neighborhood. When I was eleven and my brother was eight, this lady, Anna, who lived on the same street as us, came to our house to beat up my mom for messing with her man. Her "man" was also my mom's man, Lonnie. She had threatened our mom in the past. This time, however, we jumped on her when she jumped on our mom. As she came straight for our mom, I grabbed a pair of pliers and my brother grabbed a hammer and we managed to get her off before she could do much damage. The same thing always happened to my mom, and of course she let Lonnie come back, as so many women do after they have been mistreated. As a young girl, seeing my mom consistently being abused showed me that it was accepted.

My mom did the best she could and I won't blame her for that. She was a young mother; by the age of nineteen, she already had three children with my father. She was a white teen trying to raise three Black kids on her own in a society that was unaccepting of her or their family unit as a whole.

Carefully Consider This...

It might occur to you as you read this that your childhood was riddled with messed up behavior too. Like me, you too were a follower, not a leader. We are very impressionable as children, and we will do anything to fit in. Try not to be frustrated by your childhood experiences. Understand that you only did what you knew. Being older and having more knowledge, you should do better now. The lessons you learned then can be passed on to future generations. The change must begin with you. Despite inevitable life experiences, we can begin to develop ourselves so we can rise to the challenge and become a bigger and better person as a result.

CHAPTER 5
EC HUGHES

I never wanted to accept that I was Black and being raised by a white mom, made it even more difficult. Whenever my dad visited, I watched him hit my mom. I would sit on my porch when I was a young child and tell my grandma Soper I wished my dad would leave and never return because he hurt my mom every time he came around. And it didn't stop with him. As you can tell from earlier stories, my mom was constantly attacked by Black residents of our neighborhood. Many of her Black "boyfriends" beat her up as well. I don't understand why she dated physically and verbally abusive men. As a mixed child, I had a genuine dislike for Black people, "my people," because of the way we were treated. I was born into a world that did not accept me. I am too light for blackness and too dark for whiteness. I was led astray in my search for me.

When I attended EC Hughes, I felt so lost. At the time, 5th grade was on its own: you didn't go to middle school until 6th grade. I was teased a lot by Black kids at EC Hughes, especially the girls. Judy Blume wrote a lot of books that I would read, but the one that stood out the most was, *"Are You There God? It's Me, Margaret."* I was not as developed as other girls in my grade, and both boys and girls harassed me. Boys would pull my bra strap from the back and call me flat-chested. The mean girls would chant a quote from the book: "We must, we must, we must increase her bust." The other kids made fun of my hair and my clothes. Often, I wore clothes that did not match. I would be wearing pink stirrups and a red shirt with a purple sweater, as well as magenta socks. Eventually, I stopped hanging around too many people since someone was always making fun of me behind my back.

I was in fifth grade when my asthma started causing problems. It happened in PE class. We had to participate in the mile run. I told Mr. Johnson, a white teacher, I couldn't do it, but he made me do it anyway. I was afraid to even try for fear of having an attack. As I ran, I controlled my breathing. It was important to remember to breathe in through my nose and out through my mouth. Halfway around the track, I started hyperventilating. I panicked, throwing myself into agitation. I tried to calm myself, but I couldn't. My wheezing was severe, and I felt dizzy. As soon as the dizziness set in, I passed out. On a nebulizer, I remember waking up in the nurses' office.   In the weeks following the incident, I received a note from my doctor saying I could skip physical activity if it became difficult. I was very frustrated when my teacher didn't believe me when I expressed my fear. Was it because I was a Black girl? Throughout history, white people have never believed Black people when they said we were hurting.

In 6th grade, I attended Madison Middle School. I had a huge crush on an 8th grader named James. He was so handsome and hung around the popular kids. Because I considered myself ugly, I had no hope of getting his attention. My self-confidence was low. It was also this year that I challenged my mother.

Honestly, sometimes I deserved to get my butt whooped, and sometimes I didn't. As a child, I remember my mom was so mad at me that she threw a high heel at me and it landed above my eye, I needed stitches. She would occasionally hit me with the belt, leaving welts and marks, and I would have to go to school like that. For the most part, I was always trying to be a part of something and got into trouble for it.

I got whooped so much, I couldn't take it anymore. She hit me and I had to run to get away from her. After jumping onto the top bunk, I pushed her with my foot when she jumped up after me. That confrontation did not go well; she got so mad that she tore my ass up. Wow! Talk about bumps and bruises, I had plenty of them. Never again did I raise my hand to hit my mom. After all, she was my mother, and I was her child. What right did I have to hit her? I'll never forget the look on her face. Because of the stunt I pulled, I deserved to get my butt beaten down.

In my teenage years, I attended four different high schools: West Seattle, Rainier Beach, Lincoln, Marshall, and then back to West Seattle where I graduated. Starting in the 9th grade; I tried to do something different. Grandma Soper and Grandpa Karch, both white grandparents, attended Lincoln High School in Tacoma, which at that time was a predominantly black school. As strange as it sounds, there were too many Black kids, so to follow in my grandparent's footsteps; I had to submit my application saying I was white. Not Black and white, just white. So that I could attend, I moved in with a family friend in Tacoma. I was excited to attend school with my friend Cindy. I had a huge crush on her brother Dominique. He was a football player, so I tried to impress him by joining the volleyball team. Unfortunately that didn't work with him at all. I still didn't fit in, despite the school's majority Black population. For whatever reason, I didn't feel welcome. It was as if I didn't belong anywhere. Here I was surrounded by *my* people and still I felt so disconnected. I wonder why. I may have felt this way because I wasn't sure who I was or how I fit into the world. The school experience did not last long. It was my first time being away from home. There was so much homesickness in me that I only lasted a quarter there before returning to Seattle.

Carefully Consider This...

You may have also lashed out at your parents. Just like I did, you raised your hand to them. Perhaps you were bullied too as a child. What if your disrespect is a direct result of how you were treated by others in your life, including your parents? In the eyes of God, if I dishonored my parents, my days would be numbered. I also learned to ask for forgiveness. We are saved by God's grace and redeemed by the blood of the Lamb. Psalm 103:8 in the clear word Bible says, *"The Lord is very merciful and gracious. He does not act in passionate anger but abounds in unfailing love."* Don't feel bad for reacting that way at the time. In that particular instance, your reaction was justified. Today is a brand new day. Be kind to yourself and forgive others. Don't let your past mistakes hold you back from moving forward. Always treat others and yourself with respect. Act with integrity and strive for excellence. Never forget that you are worthy.

CHAPTER 6
WHO RAISED YOU?

How we are raised as children directly impacts how we live as teenagers and as adults. You gravitate toward the people you are surrounded by the most. I stuck with what was familiar to me and it didn't always work out in my favor.

All three of us were bullied a lot in the neighborhood, especially by people who looked like us. While I never felt accepted by the white community, the Black community did not want me either. As I tried to find myself, I hung out with different people to see if that helped. When I was in 5th grade I started hanging out with Polynesian kids. My brother hung out with Cambodian kids and my sister just hung out.

In High Point, I had a childhood friend who lived in a two-story house behind ours. Her Polynesian family included all her sisters, along with her mom and dad. As a result of spending so much time with her, I became one of her family members. I evolved into an honorary "Samoan" girl. It got to the point where I slept more at her house more than at mine. I envied the way her parents raised her and her sisters. I was also introduced to the discipline they used and carried that into how I used discipline later on in life.

It was amazing to learn the Samoan customs and traditions, including how to celebrate "the Fa'a Samoan way". To this day, one of my favorite Samoan dishes is "fa'alifu fa'i", cooked bananas in a savory coconut sauce.

I remember a time in 9th grade when my friend's mother was teaching me how to speak the Samoan language. Anytime I was in the house, she said, I could not speak English and I had to speak to her in Samoan. I wanted to belong so badly that I bought a Samoan/English dictionary. In addition, I bought a book called Gagana Samoa, which came with a cassette tape, which I listened to on my recorder so that I could practice. It's crazy to think that I flunked my Spanish class at school because Samoan was more important to me than Spanish.

After they moved out of the projects and into a house in Skyway, I visited often and sometimes stayed the night. We had a lot of fun and got into a lot of mischief. In my struggle with myself, I became someone else. Since I wanted to be Samoan, I made it my business to learn anything and everything about the culture. I rejected what I was to become for something I could never be.

Due to my constant association with Polynesian people, I eventually had children with two Polynesian men. Boogie and Olivia's father is half Samoan and half Hawaiian, while David and Sienna's father is a full Samoan. As an adult, sometimes I will talk and, depending on who I am speaking with, my "Samoan" accent will come out in my words, or sometimes I might say a few words in Samoan. Words like: 'ai mea leaga or tofa soifua. Fast forward into this story, and we will see that we eventually started attending a "Samoan Church". Now our pastor says it isn't, but when 75% of the congregation is Polynesian, it seems that way.

My brother found refuge with Cambodians. Eventually, he was able to speak Cambodian almost fluently. His favorite Cambodian dish was fish head soup. Ultimately, he joined what is known as an Asian Blood Gang. His identity is partially shaped by his Cambodian family, who just happen to be gang members.

Growing up, my sister went through a lot, especially since I was such a bully to her at a young age. I didn't treat her like a sister at all. When she was thirteen, our family was involved in one of the first cases in our state where a child divorces their parents and ends up in foster care. While she had never belonged to a gang per se while growing up in foster care, she had belonged to the church of Scientology, which is a cult-like group that manipulates young minds.

As you can see, we each struggled to figure out who we were in our own way. To find identities that we could never truly claim as our own, my siblings and I gravitated toward another race or culture. When our family did not take the time to pass on traditions and teach us the way of our ancestors, we found families from other cultures who did. But given our mixed cultural background, what heritage did we receive? At this point in our lives, nothing.

It was unclear what our family history was. Unlike other families, ours had no record of our ancestry. Stories weren't handed down from one generation to the next. Having lost all of our elders, we had to figure this out on our own. It matters who raised you and what your upbringing was like. Traditions must be passed down from generation to generation. Sometimes you may have to create new traditions in your family that you pass on to future generations as well.

Carefully Consider This...

It's possible that you have struggled with your uniqueness as well. You adopted characteristics and mannerisms that weren't yours. You tried to fit in with people who weren't your own. Don't worry. It's okay. We are all human at the end of the day; we gravitate toward the energy that pulls us in its direction. While we cannot choose our biological family, we can choose our emotional ones. The emotional family members we have chosen taught us life lessons both good and bad, that we will pass on to future generations. Through those connections, you feel an unconditional love which sustains you through different phases of your life. Don't forget to pass on the traditions and values you learned. By understanding each other better, we can always make this world a better place.

CHAPTER 7
SIBLING RIVALRY

We firstborn children are expected to set a good example for our younger siblings. Sadly, the example I set fell far to the other side of that spectrum. In High Point, my sister and I shared a room with bunk beds, and my brother had his own room. Since, I didn't like my tattletale sister I made her sleep in my brother's room while he slept in ours.

As a momma's boy, my brother was spoiled rotten. He thought he was a mechanic and took doors off hinges. He was always getting into our mom's things. When he was about ten months old, he got into her purse and put mascara all over his eyes. He never got whooped. I remember an incident he had when he was five; I knew it was finally his turn to get his butt whooped. As I chased him down the hall, he jumped through the window. Following him, I tackled him, and he pierced me in the back with a pocket knife so he could escape. He got away just fine– with everything!

Growing up, we had a very dysfunctional childhood. While hanging out at the Girls Club of Puget Sound, my brother teased my sister, saying some hurtful and mean things. She grabbed a knife from the kitchen and chased him around the building, trying to stab him if he didn't shut up. Even though she never caught him, all the kids were on high alert watching from the window. A staff member went outside to resolve the problem. What is it with us and violence? I think it was a direct reflection of the environment around us. We didn't know what calm is like.

As children of five, six, and eight, we used to go around our neighborhood and find dead animals. We would bury them in our front yard after bringing them back to our house. Then, we would make crosses out of little sticks that we found and have a small funeral service for the dead animals. It was our way of bringing peace to these animals since our home was full of chaos.

As children, we attended High Point Elementary School. On our way to school one day, my cousin suggested we play a game. There were four of us myself, my sister, and my two white cousins (one my age and one my sister's age). My sister and my small cousin were both in kindergarten. We made them pull their pants down on the way to school. When we got to school my sister told the teacher, who told the principal and I got whooped with a wooden paddle in the principal's office.

During our teenage years, my sister and I hung out with some childhood friends in Skyway. My brother was talking trash to my sister and she did not like it. Together with my sister and me, Cora, Dinah and Sefina gave my brother the beating of his life. Using fists and sticks, we beat him to a pulp. Despite being siblings, we fought like enemies. Where did we draw the distinction between being siblings or adversaries? We operated from a broken place. We weren't protected when we were bullied, so we sometimes took it out on each other.

Another time, my sister and I caught the Metro bus to school. The 106 bus took us from Skyway to Rainier Avenue. She was probably twelve years old and I was fourteen. We were seated at the back of the bus, one on each side. As these popular kids got on the bus, they started talking nonsense to my sister, and I didn't stand up to them. Because I wanted to belong, I allowed them to make fun of her by acting as if I didn't even know her. She was pushed to the point of tears and I did not do a thing, like a big sister should have. I also failed to protect my brother. Some of the time, it was me who led them down the path of destruction. Was I your sister, friend, or tormentor?

I'm not saying it was always bad. You can find the good in every situation if you look for it. We did have a lot of fun. We played kickball with our friends Marsha and Charlene on the huge field across the street from our house. We invented games by wrapping ourselves in a huge blanket and rolling down the hill in front of our house with Nina and Cora. That's what we called ghetto fun. It was our own version of a theme park and we were riding a ride. Red light, green light was another game we played outside. In our area, we took part in free lunch programs and Easter egg hunts. As a child, the free lunch program had a profound impact on me, and I always hoped when I grew up I would also give back to the community. We often played at the park down the street from our house. As children, we used to get up every Sunday morning hoping that our mom would take us to church. She was depressed some days, but other days when she was able, we would go to Sunday school to learn about God. As a ten-year-old, I participated in a fashion show with the Girls Club of Puget Sound. Having been involved in that show, I was able to look at myself differently; for a moment, I was beautiful. There were many activities we did with that club, and it kept us out of trouble.

My brother and I first accepted Christ into our lives when I was ten and he was seven. Aunt Elena took us to see a Billy Graham crusade down at the Kingdome in downtown Seattle (now known as Lumen Field). I was delighted to listen to him teach us in such a simple and loving way. He drew me into Jesus' story through his charismatic way with words. When Reverend Graham called for repentance, my brother and I raised our hands. Walking down the center stage for prayer, I felt a sense of peace wash over me. Although I wasn't sure why I felt that way, I knew something had changed inside of me.

Sometimes it was music that brought my siblings and me together. Our neighbor, Daniel, was a gifted musician who loved to share it with us. He even took the time to help each of us to write our own rhymes and raps.

Here's an example:

Mine:
Well I'm lady K and I'm here to stay, I got a lot of conversation for the men of today.
Well I am kind of short in my leather boots, that's why the guys say I'm cute.
When I walk down the street all the pretty boys look, they want my number in their telephone book.
I say no and that's a fact because I'm a young lady and I don't do that.
Well I have to go and I'll let you know that Tyson T will rock the show.

My sister: (according to my memory)
Well my name is Celeste, I wear a pretty dress and let me tell you one thing,
I don't take no mess,
With my big black eyes and my sexy thighs, that's why I get all the guys.

The way my sister remembers it:
Well my name is Celeste, and I am the best
I am the prettiest girl in the Northwest...

My brother:
Well I'm Tyson T with my bebedees,

When I rock the mic you can't mess with me...

Even though we acted like strangers and enemies sometimes, we were extremely involved when we wrote our rap. It taught us to work together effectively through our shared interests. In our own unique ways, we loved each other. What we didn't learn was how to show it. Today, we continue to work on being more loving toward each other.

Carefully consider this...

Your family may have been full of flaws too. You and your siblings may have fought because that was what you knew. Perhaps you weren't taught to love each other just because you were family. Blood should always be thicker than water and our loyalty to family should always come first. There may be some things you wish you could take back. You made amends when you realized your mistake. You can ask for forgiveness from the person you wronged and improve your ways. While you can't change the past, you can focus on the present for a brighter future. Improve your relationships today. Choose your words carefully. The words that taste bitter to you are almost certainly toxic to the person with whom you are speaking. According to Proverbs 4:24 in the clear word Bible, *"watch what you say and how you say it; always speak the truth and never with hostility about anyone or anything."* Let's encourage and lift each other up. By doing so, we make this world a better place for those who will come after us.

CHAPTER 8
CRACK IS WACK

My dad exposed me to the drug game for the first time when I was a preteen. There were a few times that we saw him, and this was one of them. It wasn't unusual for my dad to sell weed, as his mom, my grandma Jeanette, was the weed lady in my old neighborhood High Point. The story I learned from my uncle Pookie is that when he was ten years old, he brought weed home to his mom, and she took over the business my uncle started. Rumor has it, people could buy weed with food stamps.

Back then, food stamps were tracked by serial numbers on the paper coupons matched to the booklets they came in. We had to have the store clerk watch us tear the money coupon out of the booklet when we paid for our groceries in most places we shopped. I'm not sure if that was a law governing food stamps but I believe they could only be sure they were yours if they saw you tear the vouchers out. I remember shopping at Earl's Corner Store and Height Point Mini-mart in my neighborhood with those damn food stamps. When I was a child, I was embarrassed having to use food stamps; nowadays people have an EBT card (Electronic Benefit Transfer). For those of you who don't know what that is, it works just like a debit card but you can only use it to buy food. EBT cards are not stigmatized like food stamps used to be.

We were at my dad's house that day; Freddy Jackson singing *"You Are My Lady"* was playing on the boom box. I was in charge while he ran some errands. He showed me a drawer where he had left two dime baggies of weed to give to customers who knocked on the door and gave the code word, "grass." I needed to open up the drawer for the consumer, and they chose whichever baggie they wanted and then dropped the money in the drawer.

At the sound of the first knock on the door, my heart started racing because I didn't want to mess up. I answered, "Who is it?" and they replied with the code word. As I opened the door, I pointed them to the drawer. To avoid eye contact, I kept my eyes lowered to the ground, which eased the transaction. After opening the drawer, they took the bag they wanted and dropped their money, then left. At that moment I felt important, because I was taking care of business for my dad. I had full control and wanted to handle it correctly. Early exposure to drug dealing led to a bunch of other trials and tribulations later on in my life, but thanks to God I learned from them.

Shortly after visiting my dad, I was living with my grandparents in Burien. My mom had kicked me out. We got into an argument because I didn't like what her boyfriend Edward was doing, and she told me I had to leave. His behavior was manipulative and abusive. When she chose him over me, I felt completely left out and unwelcome. She should have listened to me and taken my feelings into account. Unfortunately, I didn't matter to her.

When I was fifteen, I decided to make some fast cash by selling crack cocaine. The group I was hanging out with dealt drugs as well. Shannon was a dude that I used to mess with and he was always out slanging. Whenever we met up, he always had a lot of money and nice things and I longed for those things too.

So far, I had always been a follower of the crowd, never thinking for myself. One of my family members used to be a "big time" dope dealer down in T-town back in the day. I would go to him with my money and double up. That is, I would give him $100 and he would give me $200 worth of product to sell. I don't know how I managed to work at a fast-food restaurant and attend classes all while hustling, but I did. At night, I'd hang out on Rainier Ave and South Hudson in Seattle, as well as 2nd and Pike by the arcade downtown, probably playing Bubble Bobble and Ms. Pac-Man.

One night some homeboys and I were up on 100th and Aurora Avenue in Seattle slanging dope, when one of them yelled "One Time!"   We knew the slang term meant that police were in the vicinity, so we sprinted in the other direction, but they caught us on a corner. When the officers ordered the canine on us, one of the dogs latched onto my leg because he smelled drugs on me. I jumped up and down, screaming to the police.

"Call the dog off!" I yelled.

The officer responded, "Stop resisting and stand still."

I threw both hands in the air and said, "I surrender."

When I stopped moving and stood still, the officer called the dog away. His teeth punctured my calf, and blood was dripping down my leg. My leg was throbbing, and I needed to get bandaged up.

As a minor, I was detained, taken to the precinct, and my parent or guardian was contacted. Because the male officer couldn't search me without a female officer present, I still had the drugs on me. As soon as I asked to go to the bathroom, I was able to flush the drugs down the toilet. It was a miracle that I was never arrested for the drugs. That incident was one of the many wake-up calls I received while I tried to copy what others did. My grandma had to come and pick me up from the precinct and she was very disappointed in me. When she walked into the precinct, I was in tears. I had never wanted to disappoint her in such a way. She shook her head, spoke to the officer, and told me to get in the car. I was let off with a warning. As we rode home grandma was silent. She didn't say a word to me the whole time. It forced me to reflect on what I had done.

Did I identify myself as a drug dealer? Did I care that much about being in "the game"? I knew damn well I had no business out there. There was nothing you could tell me then. At fifteen, I just knew what I wanted, right? My neighborhood was filled with drug dealers and gang bangers. It was considered an honor to be a drug dealer. I wanted what they had; nice cars, nice clothes, money, and a lot of food to eat. There is nothing like the rush you feel when a client approaches you on a street corner to purchase your products. I tried my best to walk the straight and narrow, but the glitz and glamour lured me back in.

Carefully consider this...

It's possible you had a side hustle as well. Your circumstances weren't like mine, but maybe you did it out of pure necessity. Perhaps you didn't have a dollar to your name, and you had no choice but to hustle. I have heard it said that drug dealers are greedy criminals who profit off the misery of others. That's pretty sad when the alcohol, tobacco, and now marijuana industries do the same; the only difference is that those drugs are legal. Never forget, your business mind was gifted to you; you were just using it illegally. Now you can fully utilize this gift and use it to your advantage. Let your past experiences propel you into a more prosperous future. Make use of the talents God has blessed you with. After all, you are God's masterpiece!

CHAPTER 9

YOU CALL IT A GANG; I CALL IT FAMILY

I was fourteen when I was first arrested for stealing from Sears. I was ordered to perform six hours of community service and undergo counseling. Apparently, I wasn't paying attention in counseling, or I was just getting it done for the courts because I got into trouble after that.

PSG was a gang formed in High Point. PSG stands for Pointside Strong Gangsta. Throw up that forty-four if you know what I'm talking about. Recently, I ran into an O.G. (original gangster) who told me that he changed the meaning of those letters to Perseverance, Strength, and Growth! For those of you who grew up in challenging circumstances, you already know what we've faced as Black people, both from ourselves and others!

In my preteen years, I first heard about gangs. The Rolling 60's, a Crip gang, moved into my neighborhood in High Point in 1987. I thought they were cool, and became even more enchanted when I learned they wore the color blue, since royal blue is my favorite color. I started hanging around them. I began experimenting with alcohol and weed at age thirteen. It was the thing to do in my neighborhood and since my mom was barely even visible, I did it my own way. I found some people who would accept me and let me be a part of their family. It would be hard to call the gangs up here in Washington State "hardcore." At that time, they were considered "wannabes," mirroring what they heard the gangs in Los Angeles were doing. (Wannabe gangsters pretend to be gang members when they aren't) Was my identity looped into gang membership? I was such a confused young lady and I wanted to belong so badly, that I even put a homemade tattoo on my arm, (the letter "C" in a heart). Although I would say it was meant for my name, it really stood for my love for the "Crips."

After six months of spending time with my new family, one of the homeboys from Rolling 60's, was shot and killed by a rival gang member in the Central District of Seattle. His memorial service was held at the funeral home on Rainier Ave and South Henderson. The sight of him lying in a casket made me sick to my stomach. As I walked past him, paying my respects, I suddenly felt queasy and a bitter taste formed in my mouth. I wanted to throw up. It was the first time I had seen a dead body. The color of his skin was two shades lighter than normal, and he looked bloated. I couldn't believe we shared the same social circles and attended some of the same parties and now he was gone. Even though that experience opened my eyes to what was happening, it did not stop me from hanging around gang members. They felt like my family, and I was at home with them.

I started dating this guy, Tilly, who was from BGD (Black Gangster Disciples). As a result, I considered myself a GD – gangster disciple. In fact, I went so far as to have my tattoo changed to a "G" in a heart balloon. Whenever people asked me what it stood for, I would say that it stood for my middle name, Gwen. To gain acceptance, I tattooed the phrase "RIP Shug" on my left hand, for a G.D. (Gangster Disciple) who was killed in Chicago. Back then, my dumb ass didn't even know who he was; I just wanted to be accepted however I could. This was later covered up by a sloppy heart with the word CAT beside it, this too has significance. CAT is what my homeboys from Mad-Pak called me. They also called me Crybaby. My many nicknames made it difficult to discover my true self. In addition, I have a tattoo of a messed-up six-point star on my right hand. It also symbolizes BGD. It stands for Love, Life, Loyalty, Knowledge, Wisdom, and Understanding.

The moment you join a real gang, you're committed and connected to that ONE gang. In my youth, I learned that you have to be jumped in, beaten down, sexualized, or commit a crime to obtain gang membership. Changing sides or jumping ship is not allowed; or rather shouldn't be done because you could lose your life. Are you familiar with BLOOD IN, BLOOD OUT?[5] It means to join a gang, you must kill someone, and to leave, you must be killed. For me, I was socialized into gang culture. Here I was already a part of two different sets, but the story didn't end there.

Although I can't recall which gang I was with, I do remember hanging outside of Southshore Middle school in South Seattle when these fools did a drive-by and shot at us. We hid behind a white cement wall to avoid being hit by bullets coming our way. You would think I would be deterred by that incident, but I wasn't. Eventually, I felt disconnected from the group and no longer felt like I belonged in part because I was no longer dating Tilly or hanging out with Shannon. I then began kicking it with my Polynesian brothers and sisters.

The "Mad-Pak" gang we grew up with sported the gray bandana and were based in my town's High Point neighborhood. Mad-Pak stands for Masters are Destroying, Packing, and Killing. In general, Mad-Pak was beefing with everyone; particularly a Polynesian "Blood" gang known called UBN (United Blood Nation).

---

[5]

I was involved in two drive-by shootings while I was associated with the Mad-Pak gang. The first happened one afternoon in July 1992. I was with two of the homeboys, Sika and Afa, when an order was issued for us to end the threat of a rival gang member from UBN because he was a "buster." He used to be with us, but he switched sides and joined them. By definition, I was one of those busters! Because I had a license, I drove the car while Sika, the passenger, fired two shots before we drove off. My heart raced, and my palms were sweating. I couldn't believe what I had just done, but there was no turning back now.

When the neighbor saw us, he called the police and reported the vehicle we were in. In retrospect, it wasn't the best idea for us to commit a crime in broad daylight, driving a bright red car. Consequently, we were arrested and confessed to the crimes. We were never told that we should always exercise our right to remain silent. It's not our job to aid the police during their investigation. That's their responsibility. My charges included reckless endangerment one. As a result of my previous theft charge, I got a little more time added to my sentence. I served 10 days in juvenile detention, as well as 40 hours of community service, $25 in restitution, and six months of probation. During my court appearance, Grandma Soper was with me. When I was released, she picked me up. Did I learn my lesson then? Absolutely not!

The second incident occurred in January 1993. On the day in question, Fale, Kent and Tumu and I were hanging out by Fale's house. The neighbor, Mr. Reeves, yelled at Fale and me from his house about where I parked my car, and told me to move it.

He shouted, "Move your damn car!"

I yelled back, "You don't own the streets!"

The argument was heated and when neither one of us made any progress; Mr. Reeves went into his house, got his rifle, and shot directly at Fale. I froze for what seemed like ten minutes. My heart was racing so fast, and my fight or flight response was heightened. Fale was lucky not to be hit by the fired shot. After fleeing, Tumu decided we would retaliate and do a drive-by attack. Kent suggested that we call the police, but Tumu said, "No we have to get that fool!" None of us were thinking clearly at that time.

We hopped in my car and went to Tumu's house to grab his dad's shotgun and then to Fale's to get his dad's firearm. As I drove slowly by Mr. Reeve's house, Tumu leaned out of the window and fired four rounds. Kent was holding the other shotgun and it accidently went off. According to Kent, the plan was for him to watch while Tumu loaded his shotgun and shoot if Mr. Reeves came out of his house. However, Kent stated that he was holding the gun when it accidently fired and he shot atop the kitchen window, shattering it. Police found all four shell casings from the gun Tumu used, which damaged the window and siding. After the shooting, we drove away to hide the guns.

In the above incident, I was so lost that I would do anything to belong to that crowd, including driving my own car at the time of the crime. All of us were arrested, and I was charged with reckless endangerment one. At seventeen, I had three charges on my record, two of which were felonies. Ultimately, I served thirty days in a group home-type juvenile facility, paid $144 in restitution, and had nine months of probation.

I needed that wake up call. The second time around, I was able to serve my time in a group home. As a result of serving time in that place, I was able to keep my job at the grocery store. After I turned eighteen, my probation ended and I never got into trouble with the law again.

My probation officer changed the trajectory of my life. My PO's name was Mr. Reda, and he always made sure to motivate me. He showed me what I would end up like if I didn't change my ways.

Whenever I felt discouraged, he always reminded me that I could do anything if I put my mind to it. Imagine that! Making up my **own** mind. In my small world of negativity, Mr. Reda was a positive voice. Despite the fact that he was assigned to be my PO as a part of his job, he took his position very seriously. Mr. Reda helped me understand how special I was.

If I had the choice, would I make some of those decisions again? It is possible that I would. All of those decisions have shaped who I am. I have been through so much that it is easier for me to connect and relate to the many at-risk youths I encountered in my job and those I mentored in ministry. Despite not making the best decisions, I became who I am because of them. At one point in my life, I was an "at-risk" youth, and I am thankful for the people who gave a care about me. In June of 2004, I paid to have my records sealed so that I could find a good job, and because of that, I have been at my current location for fourteen years.

The scripture I love the most is Romans 8:28, stated in the clear word Bible, which says, *"We know that God is able to bring something good out of every circumstance, as long as we trust Him and remain true to the purpose for which He called us."* Even when things are bad, God made them good. I am grateful for the fact that God was working things out in the background even when I wasn't aware of it.

Carefully consider this...

You may have been involved in gangs as a youth. You may still be associated with or involved with a gang as an adult. Gangs today are quite different from those of the past. Nowadays, I know gang members who are contributing positively to society. It's no longer about the colors you wear or the streets you claim. This time around, it's about the money you're making and the lives you are changing. For the young people who are coming up, we are like a big brother or a big sister. We mentor the youth and show them there is more to life than the streets. We teach these young people about business ownership and management. Use your experiences to guide the next generation. By leading, they will follow and become better for coming generations.

CHAPTER 10
TRUE LOVE WAS SUPPOSED TO WAIT

I was a young girl with no direction and no great examples of how men were meant to treat me. I had only seen men come and go out of my mom's life. They used and abused her. The drug life took my dad away from us, so he wasn't there to show me either. My dad was eventually caught sent away for a long time. He has been in and out of prison all his life. He even graduated from high school at a juvenile detention center called Green Hill.

In any case, the rest of my family had moved to a big yellow house in Skyway, which is also known as South Seattle. We had finally made it out of the project, which was good. However, as they say, "You can take a kid out of the projects, but you can never take the projects out of a kid."

Through experimentation, I learned about sex. Nina, one of my childhood friends, once told me that sex was like candy. Once you have one piece, you can't stop because it's so addicting. I felt validated by the attention I was getting from it. I never forgot what she said to me, and I let it fester in my mind until the day I finally allowed myself to have sex. I kept having sex like I keep eating recess peanut butter cups, one after another.

There was a boy in our neighborhood that I was attracted too. He was light-skinned and with blue eyes. I thought he was so fi-ine! Birdman was his name and I thought he was the most handsome guy I have ever seen. I would steal stuff from the corner store to impress him. To get drunk with my friends in the neighborhood, I would steal liquor from the mini mart. Thunderbird mixed with Kool-Aid and Mad Dog 20/20 were our drinks of choice.

It made me feel special because Birdman was showing interest in me. That was something new for me and I craved that kind of attention more and more. When I was a child, I wish someone had told me I was pretty or stressed the importance of self-worth to me. As someone who had been bullied a lot and didn't consider myself attractive, having someone pay me such attention felt like winning the lottery. As a result of my naïveté, I let Birdman talk me into having sex with him. I was told he would give me the world if I let him have me, and we would spend our whole lives together, as if a sixteen-year-old boy could ever give anyone the world?

His pandering was a bunch of bull, but I bought into it. I was sucked in! Often, people will tell you what you want to hear in order to get what they want from you, and this was one of those times. For love and attention, I would do anything.

Instead of treating my virginity as a prized possession, as the church had once taught me, lying on a white t-shirt, I got my cherry popped on top of an elementary school in Skyway. What a miserable experience, 20-30 seconds of pain and misery, for what? As I bled quite a bit and was hurting, I had no idea of what to do.

After that experience, I was like, "Now what?" That's it? What's next?" I believed everything he said to me. He didn't care about me, just about what he could get from me. I was ashamed of what I'd allowed myself to do. I felt unworthy, and I felt dirty.

42

Although I thought I'd made a huge mistake, I really wanted him to like me.

We dated for about two months before he moved on to the next girl. Once he got what he wanted, he discarded me like a used candy wrapper. Trying to achieve something I never had, and to be someone I was not, I fell into the trap. The aim was to embrace love from a man. The men in my life had all been abusive, so I was more vulnerable to a sweet-talker like Birdman.

The first time I was hurt and rejected, I became a wild child in every sense of the word. I became addicted to sexual activity. Almost every guy I 'dated" I was having sex with, so I didn't care who I was messing with. I didn't care if he had a girlfriend or was dating a friend of mine, I was gonna get mine before he got his. However, that wasn't the real reason. I was dazed and confused, just wanting to be loved.

At the age of sixteen, I had already slept with about seven different boys. On the side of the Kmart building, I remember having sex with a Polynesian guy from the Blood gang. We found an old mattress in the bushes and got our freak on. I'd say that was some straight up hood shit. Among those seven dudes, I even had sex with two brothers from Mad-Pak although not at the same time.

It was the one way I could feel that someone wanted me, but all they wanted was a piece of me and not all of me. I allowed myself to become molded into a promiscuous girl looking for love in all the wrong places. I accepted what was spoken into me, and what I saw around all me, as my reality. My experiences growing up dictated who I became. I was a loose girl just like my mother. I mirrored what I saw and created my own versions. Sometimes I used protection, sometimes not. My life was all about getting high and drunk without a care in the world about what I was doing. I was on a mission to destroy myself.

If you're reading this, I encourage you not to always try to fit in. Be a leader in your own life, and you can make decisions that make you proud. First, you have to love yourself before you can love anyone else. We often give away things we don't have ourselves. As I tried to fit in, I continued to lose myself. At the age of 16 ½, I contracted Gonorrhea and everything changed. Even though it was difficult, I eventually confided in my grandma. It hurt to disappoint her again, but thankfully, she took me to the doctor and we caught the infection early enough to prevent any permanent damage.

As a result of the diseases going around and the threat of HIV, I was scared straight. I decided right then that I would honor my body. I had to learn how to forgive myself and move forward. In other words, forgiveness is a powerful tool that opens up doors for a greater number of things to come. In Psalm 103:2, it says, *"as far as the East is from the West, so far has He removed our transgressions from us."* When God forgives our sin, he separates it from us and He doesn't even remember it. We're the ones who continually rehearse the situations we've faced. To truly forgive myself, or someone else, I must forget the sin that I or they have committed. That act of forgiveness doesn't mean that I have erased what I have done up to this point from my brain, it just means that I have removed the ugliness from my heart. By letting go, I kept pushing forward. Once I decided not to have sex anymore, I forgave myself and moved on.

Carefully consider this...

Perhaps your path was similar to mine. As a promiscuous individual, you didn't treat your body with respect. By having sex with multiple partners, you created soul ties with them. Each time you had sex or were intimate with them you exchanged powerful energy that sometimes stayed with you. As a result of your deeper connection with them, your relationships with them may feel unique. Like me, you could feel extremely shameful or angry that you did that. It is important that you forgive yourself. Will you ever forget it? I doubt it! Keep on walking toward your healing and loving yourself deeply. The more you guard your mind, will, and emotions, the more you will be able to sever those soul ties and be completely free. According to Proverbs 4:23 in the clear word Bible, *"above everything else, guard the affections of your heart; the emotional attachments you make determine the course of your life."* Take time to work on yourself and love **you** first! Then it will be easier to give that love to the person who deserves it.

CHAPTER 11
TEEN MOM

Throughout my childhood, I always imagined that my life would be better when I was an adult – that I would never make the same mistakes as my parents. All that changed when I ignored my grandmother's warnings about taking a road trip to California with my friends Tammy and Helen. Unfortunately, we only made it to Salem, Oregon before the car overheated and broke down. I had to call my grandma to ask her for money to replace the radiator and then we were back on the road.

Jonathan and I met at Gabriela's graduation ceremony. Tammy, his cousin, introduced us. The first time I saw him; he had caramel-colored skin, stood about 6 feet 2 inches tall, weighed about 230 pounds and wore a blue bandana. He wore a hairstyle similar to the samurai warriors in Asian movies. It was bald all over except for an island of hair that he wore in a ponytail. I was captivated. As soon as I saw him, all I could think was, "Damn, he's fine" and "I'm gonna "bag" him." It didn't matter to me that he already had a girlfriend. Plus, I didn't even know him. Tammy told me he was with SOS Crip gang. For those of you who don't know, SOS stands for Sons of Samoa.

Since we stayed in California for about two weeks, I had plenty of time. All I had to do was turn on my charm, hit the weed, have some drinks, and make it happen. At the time, I didn't realize he was only fifteen years old. I only found out after we became intimate.

Still not knowing who I was, I wanted to be able to identify myself with having a "man". But this was only in theory – a fantasy I alone had built in my desperation for self-worth. In reality, I had sex with a partner and that was it. And when I got back to Seattle, it only took a few weeks to realize that I'd gotten something I had not wanted: Pregnant.

After catching an STI two years earlier, you would think I would have made sure to use protection! When you don't use your head (brain) and think with your small head (poon-poon) stuff like that happens, not to mention how drinking and getting high impairs your judgment. And there was a part of me that thought I had someone, but he never even asked me to be his woman. It wasn't a relationship, but a situation-ship. If I did not have a relationship with this little embryo's father – without self-worth or any sense of responsibility – I would be raising this baby by myself.

The day I found out I was pregnant; Grandma Soper was there to help me create a plan to get myself back on track. My relationship with God has always been strong, having attended a Baptist church in our neighborhood since I was ten years old. As a matter of fact, I sang in the choir and participated in many activities. During one of these activities, I met my good friend Cindy. When I became pregnant, one of the mothers in the church chastised and shunned me, telling me that I was a sinner and would have to answer to God. I was no longer welcome. She didn't want me to set a bad example for other youth in the church. She judged me instead of wrapping her loving arms around me, so I left the church.

Despite his occasional phone calls to check in, Jonathan did his thing and I did mine. We weren't in a relationship; hell we hadn't even formed a friendship. Trying to prepare for my baby's birth, I worked long hours at the toy store where I worked. I worked all the way up until he was born.

In April 1994, when my oldest son was born, my life was forever changed. As soon as I saw this precious human, I knew I had to love him more than I had ever thought possible. Probably a week or two after he was born, his father came to Seattle to try and make things work. My son is named after three generations of men on Jonathan's side, including his Japanese step-grandfather. After Jonathan's mother first met him, she dubbed him Boogie, after her father, a name he has carried with him all his life. In total, my son has four names from his father's side.

Jonathan and I moved in with my grandparents and started our so-called lives. I tried my best to make this work with this person, who I didn't know at all. We weren't even friends before we decided to have sex. I wasn't the first person he had sex with and surely wouldn't be his last. Now sixteen, he wasn't ready to be an instant father. There I was, expecting him to get a job and help support our new family and he hadn't even finished school yet!

Regardless, of whether it was immaturity or his overall personality, he was a jackass in every sense of the word. But I accepted it. I didn't want to become a statistic as a single teen mom. When Jonathan told me that he was naming his homeboy, Snoopy -a hardcore Crip- as my son's godfather, I let it slide. But in our daily lives, I wasn't one to keep my mouth shut, so we argued a lot. Even when he put his hands on me, I took it since I didn't want to have my son grow up without a father. One time, he shoved me so hard that my body created a big hole in the wall about the size of four basketballs. It was probably the third time he had hit me and I had had enough, so I called the police. He was arrested and taken to jail. His parents weren't happy.

I was told by his mother, that if I kept my mouth shut, none of this would have happened. "Just be a good little girl and do as he says," she instructed. "He wouldn't have to strike you if you would just listen and obey." What I found strange about that advice was that his dad had never physically abused his mom, so I can't understand why she told me to accept that kind of treatment. Jonathan was undoubtedly her favorite and was able to do no wrong. After he was released, we got back together, just as my mom did with all of her abusers. My mother had modeled abuse for me and now we are modeling it for our son.

Three months after my son was born, Jonathan's parents visited Seattle. They hadn't seen their father Tafa in a while, who lived in South Seattle. When they were ready to head back down to California, Jonathan convinced me to let Boogie go. He assured me that his parents would only keep him for a week and then bring him back home. Even though I didn't want to, I let my son go.

Needless to say, they didn't bring him back, which worried me sick. What made it worse was that I'd given my son his father's last name instead of mine. You would think I would have followed suit like my mom, who had given all of us her last name. However, I wasn't proud enough to give that name to my son, and I liked Jonathan's last name. Adding to the stress was the possibility that his parents could decide to keep my son at any time and I would never see him again. The fact that he carried their last name made it that much easier for mischief. It caused a lot of problems between his father and me, and we fought every day until he was returned, an entire month later. After thirty days of total depression, I vowed I would never give my son back to Jonathan's parents again. I would never sacrifice my needs, wants, and desires to please another.

Nine months after my son was born, I became pregnant again. During this time we had moved out of my grandparents' house and were living in our one-bedroom apartment in Des Moines.

Snoopy, his homeboy introduced him to smoking shermsticks. Shermsticks are made by dipping your cigarette into embalming fluid and letting it air dry. When it's dry, it's ready to be smoked. When you smoke that stuff, you start to hallucinate. One night, while I was six months pregnant, he was with his homeboys at our apartment. After smoking one of those shermsticks, he began hallucinating. I was mistaken for a rival blood gang, and he started yelling at me, saying "What's up, Cuz," and threatening me with a gun. With my son in my arms, I jumped out of our bedroom window and ran. He fired several rounds, and a bullet struck a big tree near me and I almost fainted. After that, I thanked God he hadn't shot me.

Then did I leave him? NO! I was working to maintain and support my family, and it was at the expense of my own physical, mental, and spiritual health.

Jonathan never did find a stable job and I could no longer afford to stay in the apartment, especially since I would soon to give birth to my second child. So we moved back with my grandparents. Despite now being a parent and working at the toy store for two years, I had not improved my decision-making skills. Before my child was born, I was stealing from customers. During the 1990's, when customers paid with their credit cards, I had to set the card on an imprinter and make a carbon copy of the credit card number. When the manager settles up at the end of the night, I'd put the carbon copies in the cash register so it's there for him or her to account for. Several of my "so-called" friends asked me to buy things for them at work, so I wrote down their credit card numbers and purchased items for them. Make people happy and they will love you, right? But the fact remains I stole from those customers by using their credit cards. In some cases, I gave the items to friends, but in others, I returned them to the store and received cash. I was desperate for both money and acceptance. The hustle was a part of me.

When my daughter was six months old, Jonathan decided to

move back to California to find work. Still willing to sacrifice to keep my family together despite the wishes of my grandma, I applied for a transfer to this same toy store in California. After my transfer was approved, I rented a 10 foot U-Haul, packed up everything I owned, along with my kids and grandma helped us drive down on a one-way trip to start a new life. Although it was a long three-day trip, my grandma made sure we got adequate sleep in our hotel rooms. Our final destination was Jonathan's parents' house in Carson.

After we had everything unloaded, I had to return the U-Haul and then take my grandma to the airport. It was the hardest day of my life. After my grandma left, I cried every day for two weeks. Suddenly, I was alone and in an unfamiliar environment. It was hard not to miss her hugs and the conversations we used to have. Her help was always available whenever I needed it, and now I didn't have that anymore. We arrived in California with nothing, so I had to apply for assistance from the state. I was awarded food benefits and a small amount of cash assistance as well as medical benefits. Nevertheless, I started work at the toy store in Torrance three weeks after we arrived and everything was well at both work and at home.

About a month after we moved to California, Jonathan and I got into an altercation outside of Ralph's grocery store. He was screaming and shouting at the top of his lungs.

"You stupid bitch!" he yelled.

"Do what I told you!" he shouted.

I yelled back, "Don't call me that!"

Someone heard and contacted the police. I will never forget the speed at which those officers pulled into the parking lot. Four cars deep they swarmed into the lot ready to handle business. We both didn't want to go to jail, so we convinced the officers it was just a misunderstanding, and they let us off with a warning. Again, I was making excuses so things would work out. I just wanted what everyone wanted: to have a whole family.

Even after four months, Jonathan was still not working or doing what he'd promised he'd do. He was hanging out with his homeboys and doing whatever he wanted. And me? I became pregnant with our third child. At this time, quite a few of us lived in his parents' three-bedroom house, and even when I managed to pay my portion of the rent to his parents, the bills weren't being paid. In order to give my kids a warm bath, I had to warm the water in the microwave and pile on blankets at night to keep them warm. Despite my efforts, I was paying our rent, and buying food with my food stamps, but it always seemed as if we had never had enough. Moreover, Jonathan continued to abuse me verbally and physically. Because we were living under such challenging circumstances, I knew I was not going to bear another child and Jonathan didn't argue with me either.

I terminated my pregnancy. Having the procedure was a very difficult decision for me, and I was very depressed afterward. Although I was always taught that abortion was a sin, I didn't quite realize the magnitude of that sin. I never understood why it was such a sore subject. During this time, I was still working and had to show up every day with a smile, as if nothing was wrong. So why did it have to come to this? To make it work, I had given up a lot, and this was how I was rewarded. I had packed up everything I owned and moved to an unfamiliar place to have a family, but I got nothing. No love, no security, and even less sense of my own identity. I'd lost myself completely.

It's custom in Polynesian culture, that when your child turns one year old, you throw a big party. It's a tradition passed down because historically there was a high mortality rate in infants[6]. When your child turns one it's a milestone that deserves a

---

6

celebration. There are lots of friends and family invited, and it's all about the baby. I was able to celebrate my son's one year BIG in Washington, but for to my daughter, we celebrated her one year in California with just our family. I felt so bad that I had deprived her of her big celebration, but I just couldn't do it. I wasn't getting a lot of work and their father wasn't working, and things weren't going well in our lives. I can see it on my face when I look back at the photos, tired and drained. As a result of my daughter's party, I promised to always throw my children parties and to have tons of fun. My family and friends were invited and a lot of pictures were taken.

Soon after my daughter's small celebration, another fight broke out. I was tired of being treated like crap and feeling like I was on my own. Jonathan's mother expected me to just sit down and shut up, but as he continued to put me in my place, he became more abrasive. After he punched me in the face one day, I had had enough. I called my grandma and told her that we needed to leave ASAP. Grandma was shocked to hear what had occurred, because I had never mentioned it in any of my letters; the only one who knew was my best friend Marsha.

Grandma bought us three airline tickets in December 1996. Even though Jonathan pleaded and apologized and tried to persuade me to stay, we left everything we owned behind and flew back to Washington with only the clothes on our backs and important documents in my purse. At this point, I was 21 years old with two children and no sense of self. All I knew was that I had to do whatever it took to take care of them.

Carefully consider this...

You may realize as you read this that you too have been abused: verbally, physically, emotionally, and/or mentally and in the process, you lost yourself. In your quest for happiness that would never come, you've allowed yourself to completely disappear. Try not to be hard on yourself. You too may have thought the abuse was normal. Your self-esteem was damaged and you were afraid of being alone. You thought things would get better if you stuck it out, but they didn't. What doesn't kill us only makes us stronger. As you heal through the hurt and pain, remember how far you've come. You are a beautiful person and deserve to be treated accordingly. Similar to the butterfly, you have overcome a terrible situation with hope, much-needed change, and a new life. Now I challenge you to walk in your transformation. You've got this!

CHAPTER 12
JUST KICKIN' IT

We were back in Washington now. Because I hadn't given two weeks' notice to the toy store in California I was unable to get my old job back, I had to find a new place of work. I was hired by a temporary agency to sort mail. It was back to square one for me – I was working two jobs, living with my grandparents, and couldn't manage to get my life together. Of course, I was working, but then I discovered the club scene. Every week, Marsha and I would be at the club together.

Since Marsha was two years younger than me, she couldn't enter the club without identification. Back in the day it wasn't hard to manipulate the old Washington State ID cards. They were thin, laminated pieces of paper. There was no type of security on those things. Cut a square where your picture used to be and replace it with another picture and laminate it again. Easy peasy lemon squeezy!!

I manipulated my old driver's license and put Marsha's picture on it. To stop the doorman from figuring out what we were doing, I would always wait for her for five minutes as she entered the club first. I normally met her at her house in High Point and we would have a few drinks before heading north. Our usual drink of choice was orange juice and vodka. Our kickin' it schedule went like this every week: Thursday's was ladies' night at Sharkies; Friday's, ladies' night at Pier 91, and then back out to Sharkies on Saturday. During a few months, this was the routine.

One time at Sharkies we were sitting in my yellow 1986 Cadillac coup de Ville. We had two other ladies, Mimi and Tasha, from our neighborhood with us and we were drinking and talking and they were sitting in the back smoking weed. My asthma was very bad when I was younger, so I mostly avoided smoking. I was deep in conversation with Marsha when the police approached from behind. I wonder how we could have missed the red and blue lights flashing. Mimi handed me the roach and told me to put it in the ashtray. Weed was not legal then as it is now.

"What are you doing?" one of the officers asked.

Mimi smiled innocently. "Just sitting in the car talking."

The officer sniffed the air. "Can I see some identification?"

The question was directed at me, as I was the driver and owner of the car. I rifled through my purse looking for my license and handed it over.

"I'm going to need you all to exit the vehicle," he said.

One officer searched my vehicle while the other checked my warrant status. My heart was pounding, and all I could think about was what would happen if he found the weed and I got arrested. By God's grace, he didn't find that roach in my ashtray. It was a small wake-up call, but how many wake-up calls did I need?

I remember another time we were at Marsha's house getting our pre-drink on; we used to mix our drinks in large cups we got from the corner store kind of like a big gulp from 7-Eleven, with a straw. On our way to Sharkies, we stopped at Skyway to pick up one of our friends. Because I was very tipsy, I shouldn't have been driving. By the time we arrived at the club, we were both drunk.

As soon as we entered the club, I made a beeline for the bathroom. I was so drunk, I fell out. We were thrown out of the club right away. Intoxicated, I hopped into my Cadillac, started my car, and drove directly over one of the parking barriers, puncturing my gas tank and disabling my car. I had to call my grandma for help, and I could hear my grandpa in the background asking, "What has she done this time?" Grandma hushed him and called a tow truck. When I needed her, she was always just a phone call away. She wanted to make sure I knew that I always had someone on my side.

My grandparents are truly a blessing from God. They served as my children's second parents. During most of my kids' lives, I worked two fulltime jobs and was rarely around for them. They were even potty trained by my grandma. My grandma would watch my children whenever I had to work. Since I was low income, she was able to receive a small amount of money from the state (DSHS) for watching my children. I appreciated that so much.

I knew I still had to get it together. Was there anything out there for me? Why did I feel the need to follow what everyone else was doing instead of caring for my children? Did I need to go out three nights a week? If so, for what? Is it worth it to get drunk, hang with "friends," and have old men attempt to pick me up? It was high time for me to readjust my priorities and focus on my children.

The last time I went out partying was when I was 22. My friends and I were drinking at a bar in DesMoines. In an attempt to compete with the veteran drinkers, I challenged a friend to many shots of Jose Cuervo. That was a mistake. By the time the bar closed, I was drunk out of my mind. I had to drive home to Burien and wasn't sure how I would get there. In a drunken state with no consideration for my own life or the life of others, I chose to drive home. With my music blasting and all of my windows rolled down, I slowly drove down Pacific Highway. Thank goodness, I was able to reach home safely. Because I was so drunk I didn't even change clothes, I just fell dead on the couch. I woke up the next morning with a hangover from hell; my head was on fire! That day, I vowed never to put my safety or the safety of others at risk for a party life.

Carefully consider this...

You may have also gone through a phase in your life that you just wanted to turn-up all the time. As a teenager or young adult, you didn't think about anything but clubbing. You didn't care about anything; hell you didn't even care about yourself! Through socializing, you temporarily escaped the woes of this world. It helped you relax and feel at ease. Don't misunderstand me, having fun is not bad. You just need to keep balance. Excitement is good, but first we must take care of our responsibilities. Enjoying ourselves should not mean sacrificing our safety. You only get one shot at living, so live *intentionally*.

CHAPTER 13
LIFE DECISIONS

In late 1997, I moved into an apartment near the old swapmeet on 216th and Pacific Highway. By then, I was in touch with Jonathan again, who told me he was moving to Washington and that he and his "cousin" needed a place to stay. After letting them stay with us for a while, my dumb-ass fell for the same old song and dance. Although it was nice to have him back with our kids, it didn't last long. It turned out that this "cousin" was actually his girlfriend. Later, I discovered she was his third cousin.

While he was living with us all he did was drink and sell drugs. He used to smoke weed before he tried crack for the first time. In the drug game, I was always taught to never get high on your own supply. You start out as a crack dealer and become a crack-head. To get some fast money, he convinced me to get back into the game. It was great - until it wasn't.

Jonathan and I started selling drugs again on Pacific Highway. We pulled an all-nighter one night, and when we went home, we didn't realize a crack-head was following us. As we slept, a crack-head broke into our house and stole all of our money and dope. In that moment, I decided that I would never sell drugs -or put my kids in harm's way- again. When you are alone, that is one thing, but when you involve your child, that is another.

In spite of all that, I wanted Jonathan to stay around so much that I did things I normally wouldn't have such as: a threesome, throwing house parties, buying him anything he wanted on credit, and allowing his "cousin" to stay with us. Eventually, the shame and resentment became too much for me and it was time for both of them leave.

Jonathan's sister moved up to live with me in the middle of 1998. At the time, she was dating a guy named Mario and she introduced me to his twin brother, Luigi. It wasn't long before we began dating. In my eyes, I thought we were together, but he never asked me to be his woman. I just assumed we were a couple since were sleeping together. Not sure why I always thought that way. It was a recurring theme for me. In my mind, I was in a relationship, but he wasn't. This became apparent when I contracted the STI trichomoniasis. I was devastated by it. It blew my mind when I came down with a sexually transmitted infection after I was **ONLY** having sex with *him*. I knew then that I wasn't his girlfriend.

I couldn't understand why I didn't deserve his love, affection, and loyalty. Why was it that I kept choosing men who treated me badly? Why did I not feel like I deserved better? In those days, I believed that if someone gave me attention, they were really into me. Why did I allow myself to keep getting hurt by these "so-called" "men" in my life? I now realize that they were men only in age; their mentality was at best teenaged. But my mentality at the time was no better. What kind of woman would continue to mess with a cheating man? Or was it really cheating if we weren't together? The lies I told myself. How many STIs did I need to catch before I woke up? But I didn't, so I kept seeing him.

Even though I used protection, a few months later I was impregnated by him. It was an IUD, which is not always 100% effective. At that point, Luigi felt he wasn't ready for children and had so much more to accomplish so I caved into his pressure to get an abortion. As a way to keep him in my life, I figured that if I did what he asked, he wouldn't leave me. Where have I thought like this before? Remember when I let my virginity be taken at the beginning of my story? Who was this woman who was unwilling to be by herself – willing to sacrifice her own needs and values in the name of being "loved?"

My grandma and I discussed what I intended to do about it. As a Christian woman, she tried to help me realize that I wasn't doing what was right, but she supported whatever decision I made.

After I had the procedure, I fell into a deep depression. I couldn't believe I'd gone through this again. I detested myself and I despised him. All I could think about was how God wasn't pleased with me and I damn sure wasn't pleased with myself either. I beat myself up, and drank to cope. My grandma was there for me to comfort me and help me through some of the pain. She made sure I ate dinner every night. She always came into the room to check on me and ensure I was okay. When I needed to cry, she was there to hold me while I shed tears.

When I saw him with another woman, I accepted that Luigi and I weren't together and I was crushed. I had allowed myself to terminate my pregnancy in the hope of keeping him in my life, and yet again, it did not work. My feelings were hurt to the point of malice. At this time, I was in school and taking a class called Human Sexuality. I learned a great deal about men and women's bodies and I used that information to put a dent in his ego. I sent him a long letter that included a photocopy of the section about men's bodies and the average-sized penis. Huh? That's what I said. Angry with him, I started messing with someone he knew. We would hook up from time to time just to have sex, and that was about it.

Ultimately, I think I made stupid decisions in my childhood and early adulthood because I was searching for something that I never received from my dad. He never showed me what a man's love was like.   I was never told me how beautiful I was, nor was I protected –basic and essential fatherly involvement that would have given me a sense of worth and a model of how I should be treated.

As a parent, I am thankful for the lessons I've learned through my childhood, and I try to instill those lessons in my own children by loving them unconditionally. I strive to be more than enough for them.

Carefully consider this...

Maybe you are reading this and have experienced the same things. By allowing yourself to have an abortion, you believe that it was murder in the eyes of God. As a result, you continue to shame yourself and berate yourself. Don't do that! Embrace forgiveness. When you make a decision like that, you can't go back. We all have a choice every single day, and it's our responsibility to make the best choice for our lives, no matter how difficult it may be.   Many of us grew up in poverty and didn't always make the best decisions, but we did what we thought was best for us at that time.

No matter what you have gone through in life, there are always lessons to learn and adjustments to make. You should never stop learning. As humans, we should always strive to become a student of life. No one ever has it all together. Never forget: **YOU ARE LOVED!!**

CHAPTER 14
RELATIONS CAUSE CHILDREN

In 1999, I moved to an apartment in SeaTac near Angle Lake. Luigi and I were still hanging out occasionally. We used to work at the airport together, and one day at work, we got into an argument. I lost my ever-loving mind when he slapped me. I told him he'd better not touch me again or he'd end up in jail. Although we had disagreements here and there, he never touched me like that again.

I decided in March of this same year to become a juvenile probation officer so I could help troubled kids the way my probation officer helped me when I was a troubled teen. I enrolled at Highline Community College to pursue an Associate of Applied Science in Law and Justice. My low income allowed me to qualify for financial aid, and that is how I paid for college. During my time in school, I worked a full and part-time job, so Boogie and Olivia were raised by their great grandparents. One year into my degree, I discovered I needed more than just an associates' degree, I would also need a bachelor's degree to be considered for the probation work. This delayed my completion date.

Towards the end of the year, I became pregnant again. Can I tell you that this dude tried to pull the bull again telling me that he wasn't ready, etc? All I heard was blah, blah, blah, no not this time. I kept my child and 40 weeks later my son David was born in July.

There I was a single parent of three children. Because I couldn't afford to live in my apartment, I had to move back in with my grandparents. Since the father of my older children never worked, I didn't receive any money from him. I was only able to take six weeks off after David's birth before returning to work and school. Even though it was difficult -or maybe *because* it was difficult- I was more determined than ever to achieve my goals.

My advice to all the single parents out there is to never feel guilty about working to support your children. Although I missed out on a lot, I am grateful for my grandparents who filled in the gaps while I took care of business. Toward the end of 2000, I got pregnant again, and 40 weeks later, my daughter Sienna was born in August.

At the time of her birth, I decided to get my tubes tied. Being a single mother, I didn't want any more children. Don't get me wrong. Had I been married or in a committed relationship I would have loved to have at least ten children, but it was not in the cards for me. Three weeks after she was born I was at work packing an order when the news came on telling us that an airplane had just flown into one of the twin towers in New York City. May all those who perished on September 11, 2001, rest in peace.

Carefully consider this...

When you read this, you may realize that you have also brought children into this world on your own. Like me, you wanted a family, but you did not go about it **correctly**. There's dating, marriage, kids and life ever after, right? For many people, that is not the way it happened and that's fine. Throughout our lives, we make a series of decisions and choices. No matter what situation you are in at the moment, always strive to do your best. When you make every effort to do well it will help you to steer clear of living with regret, self-abuse, or self-judgment.

CHAPTER 15
HOODWINKED AGAIN

Confucius once said: "Fool me once shame on you. Fool me twice shame on me," to which someone would later add. "Fool me three times and I'm just a damn fool."

In January 2003, I was in my second quarter at Central Washington University. I was completing my bachelor's degree at a satellite campus in SeaTac. My older kid's father and I started messing around again in February. He was back here in Washington supposedly doing better. At this point in his life, he had two more children from his other baby momma. According to him, they weren't together anymore and he realized how much he loved me and needed me. He was working and ready to commit to family life, but there was one stipulation: his kids were included. That was fine with me. They were my older children's siblings, and this was my chance to finally have the family that I had always dreamed of having: mother, father, kids, and a dog all living happily ever after under one roof. I allowed him and his kids to move in with us when we lived up the street from my grandparent' house in Burien. We had a red nose pit-bull named Baby Ganja (BG) until our landlord found out and we had to get rid of him.

Jonathan worked for a while and helped with the bills and other things. He would watch the kids when he was off work so I could go to work. But eventually he lost his job and stopped working. Then he started kicking it again with some of his home-boys, and the cheating, physical and mental abuse started all over again. It was then when I found out his other baby momma was pregnant with their third child. To make matters worse, he also gave me Chlamydia, yet another STI. By this point in my life, I had had three types of STIs two of them from both of my children's fathers.

My situation at the time was no different from my mom's: a single mother of four children. I was terrified. My mind went back to how we had grown up and the things that had happened to us. When I saw the way my mom was treated and how we went without basic necessities, I knew I couldn't let that happen to my children. Look at me, I was working, attending college, and raising my kids. Yet I always went back to what felt familiar to me. No matter how toxic or painful somehow I deemed it as safe because it was all I'd ever known. What I hadn't realized was how Jonathan's constant reappearance in our lives was affecting my kids. They heard and saw how he treated me. I was not aware just how badly that situation affected my children until many years later. So, after a year of turmoil, it was time for Jonathan and his other kids to leave. When they were gone I was able to focus on finishing school and other things that mattered to me, such as giving back to the community. It was then that our family outreach program began. During this time, my children learned the value of giving back without expecting anything in return.

My bachelor's degree in Criminal Justice was awarded in June 2004. My grandparents and I were so proud of my accomplishment. When I walked across the stage to receive my diploma at graduation, I realized how strong I was. As my kids screamed, "Way to go, mom!" My grandma was grinning from ear to ear. My grandpa Don told me after the ceremony, "I knew you had it in you." I am grateful that my brother was there to capture that special moment on film. After all I had been through; I had finally achieved my goal. Praise God!

Carefully consider this...

Maybe you too have repeatedly returned to a toxic situation. You kept doing the same thing expecting a different outcome. That's what we call insanity. Show yourself some grace for what you went through. We know only what we have experienced. Now that you've survived the rough patch, you're on your way to bigger and better things. Set yourself up for success by focusing on what you love about yourself. Always remember that success is something you define for yourself, not someone else. Never forget, the best is yet to come!

CHAPTER 16
YOU CAN BOUNCE BACK FROM ANYTHING

How many of you have ever filed for bankruptcy? What if I told you I filed two times in my life? It was all my doing the first time. I had so many credit cards and one of the ways I'd sacrifice to keep Jonathan in my life was to buy him anything he wanted. You want clothes? Let's charge it. You want a new TV? Let's charge it. You want a car? Let's charge it. I had debt coming from my nose, ears, and eyes.

My grandma had always told me to spend wisely and not live above my means. She advised me to use credit responsibly. When I was a young adult, being responsible was the last thing on my mind. I bought so much on credit and accumulated so much debt that I had no choice but to file for bankruptcy. In 1999, when I was 24 years old, I filed for bankruptcy for the first time. Sadly, I only filed on about $60,000. When I look back on that now, I could have paid off my debt if I had been determined enough.

Let's fast forward to 2006. At that time, my credit was better, and I was working for my uncle and earning $18 an hour, which was a lot. Ownership was discussed about a lot in our ministry, and I was approved for a loan to buy a house on the West Hill of Kent. In May 2006, we closed on our 3 bedroom 1 bath home for $245,500.00. It was a mystery how I was approved for that type of loan on my income. It was such a wonderful day for my family. In those days, I had custody of my niece and raised her with my kids.

Remember the housing crisis of 2008? As it turns out, the loan I was approved for was an 80/20 loan, that means you have two loans. The first loan covered 80 percent of the home's cost, and the second loan covered the remaining 20 percent. These types of loans were predatory and I should have never have been approved for them.

As an added bonus, I was now supporting my dad, who had just gotten out of prison and had recently moved in with us. When my dad moved in, my uncle, (my mom's brother) decided to let me go because he didn't like my dad living with me. Two years after I started working for him, I found myself without a job. Having cashed out my 401k from my previous employer, I was able to stay afloat for a few months. When I asked the mortgage company for help, they told me we had to be behind to receive help and, up to this point, I had always paid on time. For the first time in my life, I was punished for doing the **right** thing! I owed more than our home was worth, and I couldn't afford to pay it off, or get another loan without a job.

It was only worth $187,000 according to the appraised land value back in 2008, and I owed $230,000, making me upside down on the loan. The pressure I was under led me to make decisions what would later hinder relationships, such as becoming intimate with a friend and falling in love with a coworker.

We stayed in the house for as long as we could until we were forced to move. Fortunately, we found an apartment in Kent that was willing to take a chance on me and we lived there for about two years. I was working three jobs just to maintain and keep a roof over my family's head. Regardless of where we lived, grandma would come over every morning to wake up her great-grandchildren and get them ready for school. This was a daily ritual until she was diagnosed with Lymphoma and had to slow it down. When she started chemotherapy treatments she was very weak. She wasn't the vibrant lady that I loved so much anymore. I couldn't imagine my life without her. I sent up daily prayers on her behalf, asking God to heal her. I cried every night worrying about her. During her fight for life, I tried to keep my mind in check. Despite battling three types of cancer, my grandma ended up healing from them all.

I was volunteering a lot in ministry to try and keep my mind off of losing our home, but I was also feeling extremely stressed. At that time, I had a close friend who was going through her own situation. We spent a lot of time together, going to movies, playing pool, or just kicking it at one another's homes. As we were talking one day, she confided in me that she had feelings for me. She told me all the things she liked about me and how much she admired me. I didn't know what to make of it since I had never been attracted to women like that.

To cut a long story short, I allowed myself to be intimate with her in more ways than one. Back then, I made an error in judgment. She wanted us to be more than friends, and that was not something I could do. I should have never allowed any of that to happen, but I did, and it did not turn out well. Not only did it ruin a great friendship, but I also felt very shameful. As a result, I felt as if I betrayed God, since the Word condemns homosexuality, but I also felt as if I'd betrayed myself too. Who was I to seek intimacy with a woman? It was a mystery to me.

One day I was yelling and crying and just out of my mind and one of my kids asked me, "What the heck is wrong with you mom?" That day I broke down and told him what I had done. My heart broke seeing his disappointment. He reminded me that I am a deaconess of the church, a mighty woman of God and I am held to a higher standard. I am not allowed to make mistakes; I have to be perfect all the time. It was like God was standing there with his scoreboard, keeping track. Whenever I made a mistake, he would add another point to the board. There is not one person on this planet who can reach that level of perfection. It was a hard pill to swallow and was not easy to live up to. From that day on it was like I needed to put up my wall again and learn to be stronger than ever! I made sure I did not put myself in any compromising positions like that and got deeper into my Word. I refused to listen to any music that did not glorify God and had to keep my spirit in check.

I filed for bankruptcy a second time in 2009. I was so afraid that the mortgage companies would come after me for the money I owed. After all was said and done, I filed Chapter 7 bankruptcy on $285,000. After I filed for bankruptcy, I had to start all over again! It took me a while to rebuild my credit. The house was eventually foreclosed on August 31, 2010, which further damaged my credit score. Our apartment complex wanted us to sign another year's lease and raise our rent, but I wanted to buy another home. After losing our home, I felt like a failure, and I wanted to pass ownership on to my kids. Homeownership is one of the best ways to build generational wealth. I felt in my spirit that it was important to own our own home. In June of 2012, Boogie graduated from high school and in July, we lost our grandpa Don. Boogie began classes at Green River Community College in September. For a short time, we moved back into my grandma's house at the end of 2012. I had reestablished my credit and worked at a good job, but I still wanted to provide something for my family. Although I didn't know it at the time, my grandma's house was also going into foreclosure, due to my uncle taking out equity loans on her home, and now it was upside down. Eventually he fell ill and wasn't able to pay back any of the money.

I tried to get a bank loan in November of 2012. We had looked at so many houses and had chosen the one we loved the most.

After paying for the appraisal and inspection, we were ready to move forward, but it wasn't meant to be. According to the law, one had to wait three years after a foreclosure before purchasing a home. The bank should have known this before accepting my money, since the money was non-refundable! Such jerks!

As a mother, that was a very difficult situation for me. It was getting closer to the time when we would have to move, but we had nowhere to go. It was necessary for us to move our stuff to storage at the end of May 2013. We needed a place to stay temporarily until the three years were up and I could buy a house. We are so thankful to my friend and sister Francine for opening up her home. Francine runs a home daycare, so we could only be at her house when her business was closed. All five of us stayed in one of her son's bedrooms. We needed to leave the house before 7 am and wouldn't be able to return until after 5:30 pm when her daycare was closed. We would sit in our van a block away from her house until we got a text telling us she was closed so we could come in. Due to her stipulations and a full house with her family, it wasn't the ideal place to stay. While it was a stressful time for us all, I was so appreciative. All six of us stayed in that room, including my niece. We are so very grateful to Francine, and her family, for making it work and for opening up their home to us. Olivia graduated from high school in June and left for college at Washington State University.

I truly believe you reap what you sow. As we lived in our apartment, we opened the door to a young mother and her son, whom we did not even know. She is now married with a family, but she got her start with us. Throughout our lives, we have always opened our home to others and it has paid off. God deserves all the glory, honor, and praise!

On December 28, 2013, we were blessed with a new home on the East Hill in the city of Kent. Who says that a nightmare can't be turned into a sweet dream? I purchased a bigger house for a lesser price and with a solid loan. After two bankruptcies and one foreclosure, I went from being houseless and couch-riding to becoming a homeowner!

Carefully consider this...

You may have allowed yourself to be intimate with someone who you knew was never for you. All of us make choices in life, and the consequences of those choices are our responsibility. Ultimately, love who you want to love. What you desire is your business and no one else's. As comedian Flame Monroe has said, "your identity lies in how you feel, your sexuality lies in who you desire, and who you are in gender is a fact." Do you booboo! Be true to yourself and do what makes you happy. Remember that happiness begins on the inside.

There were so many events that happened in between, but the key is to never give up. Our identities are sometimes equated with things, and when those things fail, some of us never rise again. You are so much more than the things and money you posses.

Will there be ups and downs? Of course. But despite all the ups and downs, we can still feel at peace.

I would like to share with you one of my favorite scriptures. During several difficult times, I have referred to it often. Isaiah 40:31 in the clear word Bible says, "*But those who wait on the Lord and go to Him for help will have their strength renewed. They will soar like eagles. They will run and not be weary.*" *They will walk and not faint.* There were times when I felt defeated, and my world was ending. I always knew God was with me, all I had to do was adjust my focus. I knew eventually things would get better. Not everything was easy, but it definitely worked for me! Never stop striving for your goals. You will never be able to succeed if you give up. Nothing is impossible for someone who puts their mind to it. I believe in you, but you have to believe in yourself as well! I know you can do it!

CHAPTER 17
I'M SOLD OUT

In April of 2004, a family friend of ours invited us to attend an Easter event at a church in Kent. There were lots of people, candy, baskets, and eggs. During this event, I heard a beautiful sista named Minister Dee pull down a fire word from heaven. My heart was touched by everything she said, and we joined the church known as Full Gospel Christian Fellowship the very next Sunday. After rededicating my life to Christ, it was on and popping. We never missed a Sunday service until the pandemic of 2020. I immediately got involved in the ministry.

In my first few months of attending, I joined the care ministry, which made sure people who got saved got what they needed after they left the altar. My kids and I made the candy leis that were given to the new members. Within a few months, I was appointed to start a ministry for singles and began organizing outings and Bible studies specifically for them in the church. Most of us were single moms, and that is still true today. I believe that as single mothers, we sought out the church as a guide for our children, especially if we had sons, in the hopes of finding positive male role models. While studying the Word of God, I felt empowered to teach a lesson to these women. My messages would focus heavily on the strong women in the Bible, like Rahab, the woman at the well, Ruth, and the woman with the issue of blood. I was looked up to by some of these ladies because of what I had accomplished as a single mother.

My children made their Christmas play debut at the end of the year. As a mom, I was so proud to see how much they loved God and how involved they were. Sometimes, we watch old videos and are amazed at how far they have come. I was ordained as a deaconess in the ministry in March 2005. By that time, the church had changed its name to Sould Out Christian Center. Deacons and deaconesses play a vital role in the ministry, in case you didn't know. They serve the attendees wine and bread during the monthly Holy Communion service. In these positions, a person should have a thorough understanding of all activities in the ministry and have the ability to function in all departments when needed. In cases where the sound man or children's ministry teacher is unavailable, a deacon or deaconess can step in and ensure that the service will run smoothly. While watching me receive my deaconess certificate, my grandma's eyes were filled with tears. She had always wanted our family to join and become active in a church. That gave me the push I needed to get closer to God. My involvement in ministry increased. During this same time, I bought in an expensive camera and began my job of taking pictures of events for our weekly bulletin. As a teenager, I have always owned a camera. Who remembers the Polaroid cameras? What about the disposable ones? I had them both. You had to take a trip to the drug store to get your film developed. With today's Smartphone's, people are able to take pictures at any time, and print them at home with ease. Whenever we look at our photo albums, they remind us of so many things we did as a family and in ministry.

From the moment we became members, my family was actively involved in the ministry. According to my children, they had no choice. I agree with them to an extent. As a Kent resident, I appreciated the church's many outreach activities. My children saw their very first Luau at our ministry, thus learning about Polynesian culture for the first time. It is so important to know and understand your traditions. By learning to understand their customs, it gave them pride in who they were while giving back to our town. I strongly believe in uplifting and encouraging people in my community. If they win, we all win. Think about it, my family was drawn to Jesus, by the church's Easter event for the city. In August of 2005, we attended our very first "Vision Conference" in San Francisco, California. We piled all nine of us in our 2003 Dodge Caravan, including two of my nephews, a friend, and her daughter and drove thirteen hours to our destination. Despite the cramped conditions, we were too excited to complain. I took them to their first theme park after that conference!

Our ministry held a huge field day for the city of Kent in the parking lot of Kent-Meridian High School in 2006. The theme was hip-hop. It was so wonderful to see my children dance and perform for the community to bring hope and joy. Many lives were saved that day. Lots of people left the event with a belly full of food and a heart full of love.

In December 2006, our ministry's first women's conference was held in Medford Oregon. I took Olivia along with me. At that conference I shared publicly some of the things I went through as a young teen girl. I told my story about losing my virginity, my sexual adventures, and how now I was learning to love myself through ministry. I was approached by so many women after my testimony and thanked for being transparent. Several of them had also faced similar situations.

We held our annual church vision conference in early 2007. This memory stands out in my mind because of what I was going through; losing my home, my job, my friend, and worrying about grandma. Cindy was a childhood friend I had met in my youth at church. I attended a Baptist church in my High Point neighborhood and she attended a Baptist church in Tacoma. We sang at their church's anniversary. We became fast friends the moment we met.

When I moved to Tacoma for that short period of time to attend high school, we hung out all the time. I was infatuated with her brother but he just wasn't that interested in me.

As adults, we kept in touch and even attended one of our children's births. Everything we did, we did together. On the Fourth of July, we would go to Ocean Shores every year. We spent most weekends in Tacoma. Our kids were very close to each other. I threw my kids birthday parties every year, and they were there to celebrate. Occasionally, they would attend church service with us and participate in community events. She was going through some difficulty in her marriage around this time. Her husband was verbally and sometimes physically abusive. She had decided to leave him and asked me to write a letter on her behalf for the courts in support of her decision. While I should have stayed out of it, I thought I was doing the right thing.

She ultimately decided to stay, and her husband told her to cut us off because of my support in writing the letter. I can't remember if it was a phone call or an email but I remember how I felt. I was devastated. I felt abandoned, betrayed, and unloved. Having cried so much that I could barely speak, I confided in my pastor. Even though he tried to explain why things happened the way they did, it didn't matter. It didn't make sense to me. I mean, how could someone abandon me like that? Trying to make a marriage work is understandable, but to disappear completely? To me, this was painful.

After that, I struggled with depression for quite some time. At times, I felt as if I was going insane. So much invested in this friendship, this sisterhood, and then BAM! It was gone. When I lost that friendship, I felt as if I lost part of myself. During that time, I struggled greatly. It took me two years to recover from this loss. I even emailed her from time to time to check on the family, but I didn't receive a response most of the time. I began taking on more church work to fill my time. I told myself I will never let anyone hurt me like that again. My wall went up and I became rough and tough. If you didn't talk to me about God and His Word, we wouldn't have anything in common.

When a position opened up and my pastor needed a personal secretary, I submitted my letter of interest. During this time in the ministry, I was serving in three roles, the most important one being that of assisting my pastor. It was my job to schedule and attend all meetings and take notes. When he was a guest speaker at other churches in different cities, I traveled with him. I gave my ALL to the position. For outreaches and meeting to prepare for such events, I was the point of contact for our city. We participated in an event called "You-Me-We", for five years. Also, we performed a few times at Lake Meridian's 4th of July Splash.

I often took on tasks that did not even belong to me, but when I saw a need I would fill it. For example, I created an excel spreadsheet to collect the names, addresses, and phone numbers of visitors and members to keep in one place for efficiency. Another would be my photography at special events and church services. Because my kids attended children's church, I assisted in children's ministry. I have always believed parents should help out at least once a month so that those teachers can sit in the sanctuary during services and hear from the pastor.

In a sense, this was great for my family because my kids were learning the Bible and Polynesian customs at the same time. This ministry opened our eyes to a world outside Washington State. Through this ministry, we attended so many conferences in California. I would take a few extra days off from work so we could drive down and after a conference, we would go to a theme park. We've been to Great America Theme Park at least three times. I've attended church conferences in Texas, Florida, Alabama, Hawaii, California, Georgia, and Oregon, and each time learning and growing in the things of God. I had no idea I would be traveling so much. We even went to Silverado Theme Park with my mom and my kids for a small vacation in Idaho. The number of times my mom had to stop and use the restroom made that a road trip to remember. We stopped about four times during the six-hour drive.

Having the opportunity to assist our pastors made my involvement in the ministry even more meaningful. All that my pastor said was gold, and as long as it was in line with the Word of God, we would never stray from it. If I received a text from my pastor while driving, I'd respond right away, not even pulling over. It was horrible and dangerous at the same time. When my family and I were at a movie and I got a text from my pastor, I felt compelled to answer immediately. The commitment was real. When I was in Washington D.C and Marsha was with me on our birthday vacation. The ministry had a conference call scheduled for that Monday and there I was, taking notes while we were ordering food in the restaurant. In my focus on God and taking care of my spiritual parents, nothing else mattered. Marsha did check me on that. After all, we were on vacation, right?

When we first joined, I remember Pastor talked about Harry Potter and how those movies and books teach about witchcraft and different spirits that cause problems. When I got home, I threw out those and all other movies that put a fear and witchcraft spirit into us. In a women's conference, I learned that masturbation is a sin caused by the spirit of lust and should not be practiced. I now find it confusing, as I don't know why God would give me such a desire if He didn't intend for me to fulfill it. You need to release some of that pent up stress. Several young people and seasoned adults made a purity pledge in front of the church in 2005. We were taught that true love always waits for the right time. Because I was not dating anyone or having sex anyway, the pledge made sense to me. I was focused on my children and God.

I tended to my pastor's schedule, meetings, and other things for a while. Then our first lady needed help, and I became an assistant to both of them. I was juggling my family, their family, and ministry, and that was not an issue for me. God gave me the grace to balance it all. Both my first lady and my pastor were coaches in the Kent School District and were very involved with helping the youth. I joined the admin team about 2013 and utilized my talents there. There was no space in ministry where I did not lend a hand. I totally immersed myself in ministry. I held a Bible study at my house, participated in outreach events, and attended as many conferences as I could afford. I gave my heart, time, and money to help further God's kingdom. My goal in 2014 was to grow in God, so I attended five different conferences, including three women's conferences. I attended the "A Victorious Beauty" in Marina, California, in May, and the "Exceptional Women's Conference" in Sacramento, California in August. In October 2014, I traveled to Dallas to attend a Mentorship Moments women's conference with some of the ladies from our church. The keynote speaker was Pastor Sheryl Brady. It was an intimate setting for a handful of women and the ability to learn from her was inevitable. My walk with God was transformed by that conference, and I began going yearly for myself. Over the course of my night job, I led at least four youth teens to accept Jesus Christ as their personal savior. I believe that being a part of the ministry and having a relationship with God helped my children make some good decisions while growing up.

Did they always make the right decisions? No, but nothing was too bad that they couldn't bounce back from. My children, nieces and nephews were very involved in the ministry. Participating in dance and drama skits, singing in praise and worship, and helping in the Snack Shack were just some of the ways they served. All of them took part in many community outreaches. There were many different events. We even held carnivals for our communities. In April, we had our Easter Eggstravaganza. Over the summer when school was out, there was a 10-week exercise program. During the year, we held a Candy Explosion for Halloween, a turkey giveaway in November, a Christmas gift giveaway in December, and a Midnight Madness event to bring in the New Year. It was a great time, and we made a significant impact on our community. A lot of things have changed since the pandemic of 2020, but people are still being blessed.

Community outreach was nothing new to my family. I have always given back, and I try to instill that in my children as well. When they were young, we gave back to our community, by packing 100 sack lunches, I would write scripture and encouraging words on the brown paper bags, and then we would head to Pioneer Square right near the courthouse to feed the less fortunate. City of Seattle has a lot of people in need.

The first time my kids met my dad's brother, uncle Pookie, was at a family outreach in Seattle. We continue to participate in community outreach once a month through my daughter's business, LiV's Table LLC. We are blessed to be a blessing and we will never forget where God has brought us.

God was and is everything to me and so was ministry until death came a-knocking.

Carefully consider this...

Are you aware there are times in your life when you are mourning, but no one has died? You may feel sad without understanding why. I was crying because I was mourning the loss of our home, the fight my grandma was facing, and the loss of my friend. Perhaps you're weeping because you didn't get the job you wanted or lack a companion in your life. Maybe you are crying because you don't like your current situation in life. Crying allows you to release all the frustration you may be holding inside. When we have ingested way too much pain, tears are a gift from God to ventilate our souls. You shouldn't hold in your tears, or you will destroy yourself. Cry out to God and let your tears flow. If you cry out to God, he will hear you and come to check on you. In the Bible, when Hannah cried out to God while praying in the sanctuary, He heard her and answered her. Today, I challenge you to let the tears flow and let go of the pain and pressures of this world. Then you'll feel lighter and more at peace.

CHAPTER 18

DEATH COMES IN 3'S

I kept in touch with grandma every day, so when I couldn't reach her for a couple of days I got nervous. On Wednesday, March 9, 2016, I received a call that Grandma Soper was in the hospital. We rushed to her side immediately. We found out at the hospital that she had been there since Monday, and that's why I couldn't get her on the phone. I was so enraged with both of my aunts. We got into an argument in the hospital room while grandma was lying there. It was cruel of them not to tell us right away, but I think there was some jealousy on their part regarding the relationship the kids and I had with grandma.

For four long days, we stayed with her day and night. Boogie never leave her side, and it almost cost him his job, but God had other plans. I stayed as long as I could, but I had to leave. I was working two full-time jobs at the time. From 11 pm to 7 am, I worked my night job, and from 7:30 am to 4 pm, I worked my day job. I spent as much time as I could with her on Wednesday and Thursday and spent the night over the weekend.

We sat in her room telling her stories she told us. My kids sang this song, "chi-baba, chi-baba, chi-wawa, an' chi-lawa kook-a la goombah..." to her while she laid there. When they were young, grandma used to sing that song to them all the time and they have never forgotten it. The song is titled "Chi Baba, Chi Baba" by Perry Como. Her grandchildren would tell her stories about her and grandpa Don going fishing or camping together. They reminded her of the times they went panning for gold or glass blowing. She took my kids to places like Leavenworth, which I have never been to. Before she went into the hospital, she took her grandsons and Jonathan's father, their poppa fishing. At all times, there were at least two of us sitting with her. It was as if we were guarding her.

I cherished my grandma dearly. She was the only one who knew what I was going through. The love she had for me was like no other. We always found time for one another. Even when she told us not to, we celebrated her birthday every year. We made frequent trips to her apartment to bring her food and make sure she had what she needed.

On Sunday, March 13th we decided to sneak away so we could attend church, which normally lasted 2.5 hours long. Because grandma was the only thing on my mind that day, I had a hard time getting into praise and worship or the Word. The church service ended at 1 pm, and I was gathering my family to head back to the hospital, when the text came through at 1:05 saying her breathing was labored. The church we attend is in Kent, and grandma was at Highline Hospital in Burien. It would take at least 20 minutes to get back to her. I shouted and screamed that we needed to leave, but before I could get my kids in the car I got a text at 1:10 pm that she was gone.

It was as if my soul had left my body. I wanted to be there with her one last time. Be sure to let her know how much I love her. I wanted to hold her hand as she transitioned. I would have asked her to hold on a little longer.

On our way to the hospital, my children and I cried uncontrollably. Grandma meant the world to us. She taught me almost everything that I know. After the world gave up on me, she was there to pick me up. After losing her, I felt like I couldn't bear the pain. Many of our plans came to a screeching halt when she went home to be with the Lord. The home-going celebration was held on April 4, 2016. I love you and miss you Grandma Soper!

In November 2016, my mom had extreme abdominal pains and kept making doctor's appointments to figure out what was going on. Her posture was hunched over, and she had a hard time standing up straight. No matter how many times she went to the doctor, they always told her that it was all in her head and sometimes sent her home with pain medication. In my opinion, my mom wasn't given the care she needed and deserved because she was poor and didn't have health insurance. There was no way she could keep going back to the doctor with the same complaints of pain, only to be told that it was all in her head.

I received a text message from my sister on February 23, 2017, telling me that our mom had been diagnosed with high-grade invasive urothelial carcinoma with sacromatoid, or Stage 4 Bladder Cancer. For me, this diagnosis was difficult because my mom never smoked a day in her life and she ate healthily and exercised. She didn't even drink alcohol. I often wondered how in the world she got cancer. Initially, I blamed her live-in boyfriend because he smoked in the house, but she also liked to play slots at the casino in the smoking section. Can I hold them accountable for her death? We may never know.

A year earlier, I had just lost my grandma and now I'm

watching my mom battle this terrible disease. I've always been the strong one, and this time was no different. Because I had no one to lean on, I tried to figure things out on my own. Here I am, serving the Lord, working in ministry, giving it all I've got, and then suddenly these things begin happening in my life.

My mind began to disconnect and I sought comfort elsewhere. Eventually, I got close to one of my former co-workers. I worked with the youth, while he worked with the adults next door. We had been working for the same company for quite a while, and I found myself talking to him like he was a therapist or something. I truly believe we provided comfort to each other during that difficult time. We talked a lot and sometimes took our lunches together. While we ate lunch we talked about our childhoods, the neighborhoods we grew up in, the music we listened to, and just life in general. We both liked hip hop, Tupac all day for me baby! He was coming out of his situation and I was going through mine. I felt heard and seen because he paid me all this attention. We were both unable to think clearly, especially me. He and his wife were separated, but it wasn't final, so I had no business getting close to him. I was in a state of desperation, loneliness, and uncertainty. At this point in my life, I was still unsure of who I was. My early adult years, I dedicated my life to raising my kids and now to ministry, nothing in between.

At the beginning of May I was supposed to be working my night job, but instead I met Dwayne for drinks and conversation. We were deep into a discussion when we kissed, and I ultimately broke my 13-year streak of celibacy and slept with him that night. That started a whirlwind of emotional instability and insecurities that needed to be addressed but weren't. At the moment that it happened, I was shocked. He said the look on my face scared him a little. I felt like I was disappointed, sad, and fulfilled at the same time.

I considered Jesus to be center of my life and ministry to be everything. I felt that I had failed God, my kids, and myself. At the same time, I felt like I needed it as well. It took me a while to understand what had just happened, but eventually I had to push forward. I will never understand why men or women step out when they are in a committed relationship unless that is your agreement. It is hard to understand why anyone, let alone me, would allow myself to become friends, not mention sleep with a person like this. I had just lost two of the most important people in my life, I was extremely vulnerable. I suppose some things are just not meant to be understood.

After we slept together, we didn't speak for a few days, not in person, not by text, not by phone, email, or message. Nothing! I think we both handled what happened in our own way. I was dumbfounded and at a loss for words and had no one to turn to. Who could I turn to for advice? I didn't trust anyone. Throughout your life, people will continue to show you who they are. Pay attention! As a Christian or a follower of God, you are held to a higher standard, so I was already judging myself. I didn't need anyone else's judgment. I had to deal with this on my own and continue to rely on God.

After about a week, we started hanging out again and discussing our lives and the choices we have made. He made me feel incredibly special. I needed to feel important. I felt like he was in tune with me. He knew my emotions before I did. Our conversations would cover our career paths, our families, our goals, and our spiritual growth. Often, we spoke without even saying a word. That's pretty amazing, isn't it?

I felt as if I were falling in love with him. I thought about him constantly. I got excited whenever he called or texted. Whenever I saw him, I was thrilled. And when we had sex, I felt amazing. In one of these exchanges, he said he loved me, but did he really? How could he when he hadn't shut the other door? There was still a small crack in it. In my heart I knew that what was happening wasn't right, but I convinced myself that because he was separated, everything was fine. Had he even spoken to me about making us permanent? While I was in the situation it didn't even occur to me. I was just living in the moment and enjoying what I could. It was all about me.

My mom began chemo treatment in May. She was in and out of the hospital for a while. Every time I went to see her, she would apologize for not having enough money to buy me or her grandchildren things. In the hospital, my mom and I finally understood each other and came to place of healing.

"I've always thought you thought you were better than me," my mom told me.

"I thought you didn't love me," I replied.

"I didn't know how to love you, but I tried my best," she replied.

All these years my mom thought I hated her, and I thought she hated me, but we loved each other. The problem was we had no idea how to show our love. We both cried as we embraced each other. Right then, I realized that my mom did love me.

Mom was one of those people who rarely expressed her love for us. To this day, I am still working on this with my children, trying to break the pattern. Mom didn't like to be seen looking scruffy and out of place. When she was in the hospital, she hated it. Despite always apologizing for being there, she assured me she was doing all she could to get better. While grieving the loss of my grandma, I was also dealing with my mom's illness. It was a hard time. It was important to me, my kids and my ministry that I kept it together.

I was with my friend Marsha at LA Fitness in Southcenter one day. As we were doing our exercise routines in the pool, I became overwhelmed with emotion and started crying uncontrollably. My world seemed to turn upside down and I confessed to her that I had slept with Dwayne. Then I described how it had happened and my reaction immediately following. Her advice helped me process the situation. I was cautioned to be careful and to keep working on myself; overall, she didn't judge me. That gave me reassurance that she would always be there for me.

In time, my mom's cancer spread to her bones, and soon after she was placed in hospice care, which focuses on providing pain relief to the terminally ill while they await death. The hospital sent my mom to her home and prescribed her medicine for comfort. My pastor came over to her house on August 26 to pray for her and to encourage us. On September 10, I awoke at 6:45 am. I took shower and planned to visit my mom before church. At 7:10 am, I got the text from my sister that mom was gone. At that moment, my heart sank. Again, I didn't make it. The tears wouldn't stop. I felt my heart breaking all over again.

After my mom's memorial service Dwayne and I stopped seeing each other. We stopped communicating altogether. He had decided to work his own life out, which sent my emotions on a deep-sea dive. I couldn't stop crying and felt so heartbroken. In addition to losing my grandma, I also lost my mom, and now I've lost myself as well. The feelings I used to have as a young girl resurfaced; I was unlovable and no one wanted me. I had known exactly what type of situation it was and I had let him into my heart. It has been said that this was a business transaction and all I needed to do was stick and move. But I stood still and got stuck.

Following that, I began making mistakes when scheduling my pastors meetings. In the midst of my emotional turmoil, I would miss appointments, forget to put meetings on their calendars, or forget to remind them. As a result, I cried myself to sleep, feeling upset or depressed, my life had become chaotic. When I was talking with my friend Toots at work one day, she got a little worried about me. She had never seen me cry before; I was always the strong one. I missed my grandma and my mom so much. I would sit and watch the "Missing You" video from the *Set It Off* soundtrack and just cry, cry, cry. When I stopped talking to God, I knew that He was still with me. His Word says, draw near to me and I will draw near to you. The work begins with us.

I began to withdraw from everyone and everything. It was difficult for me to manage my temper with my niece and children. My children never knew the depths of the things I was going through. At one point, I was robbing Peter to pay Paul, using my credit cards to keep the lights on, food in the refrigerator, and to make sure the water bill was paid.

I never stopped attending church, putting my time in, and paying tithes like a "good" "Christian." I was still working two jobs and taking care of my kids and niece, but I was so lost. I mean **lost** – in my thoughts, my emotions, my feelings, and my spirit.

The memorial service for my mom was held in October, and I believe it was success. I had both sides of my family show up along with my church family without causing too much drama. I consider that to be the definition of S.U.C.C.E.S.S. This was especially true since my mom's family disliked my dad. Watching my dad cry was hard. The love of his life was gone, he muttered. After all was said and done, I truly believe that he left a part of himself at the church.

Toward the end of October, I attended a Mentorship Moments conference down in Texas with Pastor Sheryl Brady. Before my mom got sick, I had already purchased my tickets, and I needed a lift in my spirit. The presence of mighty women of God has always given me the courage I need to deal with my crisis. All those beautiful women praying for me during my time of turmoil gave me the comfort I needed. Pastor Sheryl Brady had just lost her sister a few weeks before the event, so she knew exactly how I felt. During that anointing service, the Holy Spirit moved so powerfully! How many of you have heard the saying with after every blessing comes testing?

I was relieved of my duties as a personal secretary via text message on December 7, 2017. A FREAKING TEXT! That was the ultimate blow. Being released when I had done so much for my pastors and the ministry when I was experiencing so much was beyond comprehension for me. I gave my all and served out of honor to God. In fact, I didn't receive a stipend until the summer of 2016, which ended when I was released.

My identity was entangled with my position. My name was always included whenever the name of my pastor or the church was mentioned. I added so much value to them with my organizational skills and my support for them, that it just didn't make any sense to me. I was hurt deeply by this. Having served with all my heart and soul since 2007, and released when I needed them most. Christians should model Christ-like behavior, and Christ helped heal people during difficult times – not turn them away.

I cried for days, wondering what I was going to do and how I was going to cope. Although I believed that I deserved an explanation deep down in my heart, I was so hurt and disappointed that I couldn't bring myself to speak about it. It felt like I had been betrayed, underappreciated, and discarded like trash. Besides my regular jobs, all I knew was serving in ministry and supporting my pastors.

Outside of being my pastor's assistant, who was I? I had no clue. In the past two years, I have experienced so many deaths; my grandma, my mom, my semi-relationship, and my position. I had to do a lot of soul-searching.

Carefully consider this...

Maybe you too have suffered many losses in your life. Perhaps you also faced depression and anxiety. These feelings may still affect you today. There will be times when we feel down and out, and that's okay. Sometimes it takes time for us to climb out of a hole that we are in. I am here to remind you that storms don't last forever and the sun will shine again soon. According to Romans 12:2

of the clear word Bible, *"don't pattern your life after this world, but let God transform you from the inside out and give you a new way of thinking."* In many cases, we're in a funk because our minds are constantly focused on sadness. To fix this, you need to shift your focus to the positive.

Today, I challenge you to remember all the excellent things about that person or situation. By changing your mind you will change your life, but it requires active effort. By taking control of the battle going on in our minds, we can accomplish anything. According to Psalm 30:5 of the clear word Bible, *"...tears may come for a night, but gladness bursts forth with the morning."* You may cry now but guarantee you will smile later. Stand up straight, put a smile on your face and walk into the new day with joy in your heart.

CHAPTER 19
LIFE AFTER DEATH

After being released, I went through a deep depression for about a month. I was going through so many emotions at the same time, and I had no one I trusted to talk to. I broke down in front of my oldest son at one point. I was at a loss for words and didn't know what to do. All I could say to him was, "How could they do this to me?" "Why would they do that to me?"

I have raised amazing children. Boogie helped me to see that this was just a bump in the road and that I now had extra time to do other things. Having more time was a foreign concept to me. I decided I would prioritize myself in 2018 while also spending more time with my kids and those closest to me. It was then I began my journey to self-discovery and making new memories.

Do you remember a time when you decided to make a change for the better and everything went wrong? The end of January, I got a call from my youngest son's school that he had a seizure. My heart sank.

David is an amazing actor. He has a natural gift for portraying any character. He was practicing for an upcoming event in drama class when he fell. It took them a couple of minutes to realize he wasn't playing. An ambulance rushed him to the hospital, and then the tests began. There were so many different types of tests done: blood tests, electrocardiograms, MRIs and CT scans. Everything was checked on him from his head to his toes.

After of all the tests, it was determined that he had a seizure due to low calcium levels. Further investigation revealed that my son was born with a genetic condition called pseudohypoparathyroidism. It is caused by changes or mutations in several different genes including the GNAS1 gene.[7] When that gene doesn't function properly, the body is unable to properly respond to parathyroid hormone, which increases phosphorous in the blood and decreases calcium. I am very thankful that my son is here with me today. As a result of that particular event, our family was indeed shaken to the core. At that time, I realized that time is the most precious commodity we have and it is important to spend time with the people we love. The journey continues...

My kids and I took a road trip to Canada at the end of February, and despite the snow, we had a good time. Driving in the snow can be tricky. The museum of Vancouver was one of the highlights of our trip, as was staying at a hotel with a swimming pool. This was our first trip outside of the country. During that same month, I taught a word at our church for Sunday service. Despite being released from my position as pastor's secretary, I still held other positions in the ministry. Isn't it amazing that God was still able to use me for edification of the body of Christ, despite all that I went through internally? My pastor asked me to teach about relationships. I discussed three types of relationships: relationships with self, relationships with God, and relationships with others. No

---

[7]

matter what you or I may be going through in our lives, if you are willing and obedient, God can and will use you. I knew, even as I taught the word, that I needed to work on my relationship with myself.

I was in need of a fresh start so in March, I cut off all my hair. Although I wanted to chop it off for some time, I couldn't bring myself to do it. This symbolized to me that I was ridding myself of burdens that had been weighing on me. In this same month, I saw comedian Sinbad live and enjoyed a movie with friends. But then death struck again. We lost Buster on April 20. He had been our family dog since 2006. That was another devastating loss. We loved him dearly! Despite losing Buster, we gained Ganja shortly after my grandma passed away, this helped ease the pain of the loss.

This was also the time when I decided to find out exactly where my family is from, mainly on my dad's side. My mom's white side is known to me, but my dad's Black side is a mystery to me. Ancestry.com's DNA test revealed that the majority of my dad's family originated from Nigeria, Cameroon, Congo, and Western Bantu Peoples. Knowing who you are and where you came from, especially your family history is important. It can be difficult for some of us black and brown folks because our ancestors were removed from their homelands and dispersed all over the world. As Marcus Garvey once said, "A people without the knowledge of their past history, origin and or culture are like a tree without roots."[8] I discovered the origin of my dads' family and now the foundation has been laid.

My dad's family hails from Brookhaven, Mississippi, which is in Lincoln County. RadieMae Stovall was my great-grandmother and she was married to John or Jonas Stovall. They had two children, my grandma Jeanette and my aunt Gladys. Maybe the people who enslaved my family got rid of great-grandpa Jonas or he passed away because my great-grandmother RadieMae remarried Dan Calcote,

---

[8]

making my grandma Jeannette and aunt Gladys stepchildren when they were eleven and twelve. There are a number of siblings from their stepfather, our Calcote bloodline, but it's not easy for me to find out any more information regarding the Stovall bloodline. Grandma Jeanette passed away in 1986 in prison. Despite my efforts, I was unable to learn more from my aunt Gladys, she passed away on September 29, 2019. According to my dad, she knew everything and everyone on both sides of the family. That will not stop me from seeking knowledge about myself and my family! The Stovall and Calcote bloodlines stand up!

Some of you might ask, but what about your mother's side? Let me explain. I can trace my Italian side back to Italy in 1874, according to my family tree. My German side dates back to 1835 to Munchen, Bayern Germany. My Swedish side dates back to 1845. In addition to hearing many of the family stories from my white grandparents, I have done a lot of research on that side of my family.

Now you see the dilemma facing some of us black and brown folks. Our people were stolen and brought here as slaves. We lost our language, our heritage, our names, and our whole identity. The federal census did not begin counting black and brown people until 1870. That's 250 years after we were first brought here. In addition, every ten years there was a new census, and sometimes the spelling of a Black person's name would be changed since people couldn't read, let alone read cursive. In the 1930 census, my grandma Jeanette's appears as Jennie L, while in the 1940 census, it appears as Jennie.[9] My great grandmother RadieMae Berry was three years old in the 1910 census which would mean she was born in 1907. Nevertheless, the 1930 census recorded that she was 21, which would mean she was born in 1909. I will continue to investigate my family history.

You can tell I love reading by the personal library I have in my room. I have two large bookcases full of books. In June, I

---

[9]

attended a book signing by, Michael Eric Dyson, one of my favorite authors, and met Angela Rye. Both of these people are very intelligent and powerful. It was an honor to sit with them and learn from them. He signed *"What the Truth Sounds Like"*, a great book. In the same month, David graduated from high school and Olivia graduated from her chef apprenticeship program with Farestart. Single moms can raise successful children, right?

I took my youngest children and niece to a WWE wrestling match in September. In October Sienna was given a certificate for her achievements in high school. After October arrived, I was in Las Vegas for four days with my oldest kids and Marsha. In November, I attended the unveiling of the Black Panther Party mural in front of the Franklin High school on Rainier Ave S. What a beautiful sight!

I'd never had the time to do any of these things before. Nor did I have the money to do them. Everything I had I gave to the house of worship. As a result of being so focused on ministry, I never took time for myself or my children outside of the church. Everything we ever did was always associated with the ministry. Who was I outside of that? The time had come for me to live my life fully.

At the end of November, I began working at my night job at the youth center, and they were having trouble getting youth into their rooms. One of the walls had a hole in it and the kids were acting strangely. They should have been their rooms by 10 pm but on this particular night, it was already 11 pm and apparently, they were on strike. They were verbally disrespectful and out of control. I went to talk to a young Black girl whom I had made contact with two nights earlier, and she lost her mind. When she raised her hand to strike me, I blocked it. Another youth jumped in and helped her put me in a chokehold. All of this was happening and none of my young colleagues stepped up to help. When two girls punched me and a boy grabbed my hair, all I could was cover my face with my hands. It took an older coworker, a 65-year-old Ms. Gracie, to snatch two of the children off of me in order for me to escape.

My experience was extremely traumatic. My mind went back to when I was child and was bullied. It was disheartening because the young Black girl did all that just make herself look good in front of some little white boy she was trying to impress. When that happened, I was clearly upset. When I calmed down, I realized she was only doing what I used to do when I was her age. Her behavior was probably the only way she knew. Eventually, the police showed up and she was arrested and transported across the street to the juvenile detention center. That was a very sad day for her and me. After that, I needed to take some time to myself.

Toward the beginning of December, I took a week off from both jobs to spend some time by myself in Seattle. I took the bus from Kent to Seattle and I spent the whole day at the Seattle Art Museum. The following day, I visited the Museum of Pop Culture. A day later, I visited the Northwest African American Museum. I only discovered this place by accident through Google. Being able to see the history of my people in Seattle was a blessing. Did you know that only one African American lived in King County, Seattle, in 1860? It was just one of the interesting facts I learned at the museum.

As you can see, 2018 was very busy for me, my family, and friends. It's possible that I kept myself so busy that I didn't have time to deal with what was going on internally. There was no time to think about anything else besides what was going on at that moment.

On the first Sunday of 2019, I attended church service with some of my Calcote cousins because my big cousin Walnut was getting baptized. It was an important event for me. As I sat there praising God, my daughter Olivia texted me that our pastor just announced me as their assistant again. Mind you, I had no idea this was even their thought. A lot of feelings and emotions arose in me that I hadn't dealt with before. I had been removed from that position, and now they wanted to reinstate my duties without a face-to-face meeting. It was as if they thought I was just sitting around doing nothing while working two full-time jobs and sleeping. Here I was, trying to find myself, discovering who I was outside of that position, and BAM! This happened! For real! I decided to calm my nerves and sleep on it. Tuesday morning, I sent a text to my pastors and respectfully declined the offer to reinstate the position. It was time to take the next step in my self-discovery.

Now that I don't serve in ministry like I used to, it's as if I have never existed, and that speaks volumes. I resigned from all the positions I held, effective October 2021. There's so much more I could say, but I'll stop here. Will we ever be close again? Probably not, as I am still trying to find ways to walk in my healing. Although I have a long road ahead, I thank God that I am moving forward. Even though that season of service is over in my life, I am still touching people through my testimony and showing them how much God loves us all.

Carefully Consider this...

Perhaps you have also been traumatized by the ministry. You gave everything you had to further God's kingdom, but it was never enough. Fear theology drove you to obedience. You were sometimes told that your wrong decisions will cause you to miss out on God's plan for your life. Occasionally, you were pressured into service out of your moral obligation to the church. It's possible you too were told God would honor you more if you gave more without realizing you were giving everything you had.

It's not about rules and religion; it's about a relationship with God. No matter how much we give, serve, or honor the church, it will never be enough in man's sight, but God is pleased. Luke 10:27 in the clear word Bible says, *"You should love the Lord you God with all your heart, your entire mind and all your strength; then you should love your neighbor as you love yourself."* The failures and shortcomings we have aren't the entirety of us; they are just a part of us. Every day, we strive to be better versions of ourselves. In the end, what matters is that we show love and encourage one another.

CHAPTER 20
KEEP YA HEAD UP

I will no longer walk around with my head hanging down. It was time to stand up, straighten up, and keep pushing forward. I had spent so much time and energy elevating others while putting myself last. I had done so much for other people, whether it was my kids, nieces and nephews, friends, other families, or even the ministry, that I knew it was high time for me to put myself first and do what I wanted and needed to do for *myself.*

In 2019, there were many comedians who stopped by my city and I loved them all. In addition to comedy shows, I enjoyed my own company at the movies. How could I expect others to like me if I didn't like myself? I even took myself out on dates. I remember going to the Bleu Note in Lakewood to support a singer I know from our hood and being intimidated to be there by myself. What would all those couples think of me? And what if I was hurt out there alone? I realized then that what-ifs will stop you dead in your tracks. If you're too afraid of what-ifs, you won't even try. Taking a chance on something by faith is the first step, and even if I fail, at least I tried.

In 2019, I took two trips by myself. I enjoyed visiting the museums in Dallas, Texas and Columbia, South Carolina. Taking public transportation is something I enjoy doing. As a tourist, I stood out like a sore thumb and almost got in trouble with some of the mentally unstable locals. I continue to travel by faith to this day. Reggie, a good friend of mine from South Carolina, told me later that I look exotic, and that is why I stand out. Particularly when I wore a tank top and flaunted my newest tattoo dedicated to my children. Whenever I travel alone, I can do what I want when I want and do not have to answer to anyone or clash with anybody else's personality because everyone vacations differently.

I received an email from Cindy in March seeking to reconnect with her. I can't describe the emotions I felt at that time. It was difficult to process what was going on in my mind. When it happened, I took two years to get over it. And now she's here 12 years later. I wondered what became of her and her family. In my heart, even though it had been so long, they were still family to me.

All at once, I felt anger, sadness, hurt, pain and excitement. My kid's reactions to hearing she contacted me were skepticism. They did not want to experience the same pain and hurt again. I realized I wasn't the only one who felt betrayed.

We met up on a neutral territory a few months later and it was a good meeting. We discussed life, love and family. We sat down a few months later and had a serious talk about how our relationship had ended. A friendship torn apart by an unfortunate circumstance was healed and restored by God. Having divorced her husband she was trying to mend broken relationships. Will our sisterhood ever be the same? Not at all, but in any case, I shouldn't harbor hatred or bitterness. As my identity was no longer defined by our friendship, it was much easier for me to begin my healing. Although she may bow out at any time, I know I would be fine because of my relationship with myself and God. As well as thanking God for our relationship, I also acknowledge that forgiveness is crucial to sustaining relationships.

Sienna graduated from high school in June 2019 and was set

to attend Howard University in August. To see my last child graduate and move up in life was such a beautiful experience for me as a mom. What a wonderful feeling to see how far my family has come from my drug-dealing grandma to my confused self to my successful children. I went skydiving with my sons Boogie and David in September. It's crazy to think that we jumped deliberately from a plane. Yes, we did, and it was incredible. During that brief moment, I felt as if I were floating in the sky with all of my angels who were watching over me, especially my mom and grandma Soper. I look forward to skydiving again with my daughters.

In 2019, I realized that my past could no longer dictate my future - especially now that I was ready to move forward. Good, bad, and indifferent past experiences have shaped the woman that I am today. In order to move forward, I had to forgive myself, forgive others, and look to God for guidance.

Carefully consider this...

Every individual on this planet adheres to their own set of moral codes. You must make the best decisions for you and your family. Your choices may not always make sense. You may not get it right on the first try, but if you keep trying and put one foot in front of the other you will eventually succeed. You stand up straight with your head held high, and walk into the room like you own it!

There will be no more tears shed for the things of the past. I have learned from every decision and event in my life. A few of these lessons I have learned repeatedly. Have you ever experienced that? You keep repeating the same things until you reached a point of understanding and have made the necessary adjustments. Each of us is born, lives and dies. The question is what did you do while you were alive? Each day you are given is another chance to learn and grow. When my time comes to leave this earth, I hope that I will have had a positive impact on the people I have met along the way.

CHAPTER 21

LIFE GOES ON

This part of the story makes my heart race. On December 31st, at 12:45 pm, I was in another department's supervisor's office discussing our New Year's plans and other work-related concerns. Usually we would talk about life, but mainly about our Sunday services and what the preacher said. When you get to know me I'm a cool cat, and when we have something in common to talk about, we can talk for days. When I turned to leave, he asked me for a hug, which I didn't think anything of because I often gave side hugs like my mom used to. As I was leaving, he planted a kiss on my lips and told me how much he missed me. I froze for what seemed like 60 seconds before turning and running out of the office. I couldn't believe what just happened. My heart was pounding so hard.

As soon as I returned to my office space, I texted my friend and coworker Toots. My hands were trembling with worry. From her response, I knew she wasn't happy. Tears began to fall and I couldn't control my emotions. I couldn't understand why he would do that. As a married man in an upper position, he forced himself on me. I started to go back over all of our conversations and realized he had been inappropriate for a long time. I just didn't take him seriously.

After texting Toots, I texted my daughters, who were angry and shocked at what had happened. Since one of my sons might go to my job and snap his neck, I knew I couldn't tell them. After being off for the New Year, we went back to work and I avoided him. The sight of him filled me with rage. My friend Marsha and I discussed the situation over the phone. She urged me to confront him and take my power back. She instructed me to speak my mind clearly and professionally. Once I confronted him, she told me, I wouldn't have to duck and hide, nor would I have to walk on eggshells when I saw him. Eventually, I was able to confront the situation and regain control.

Ladies and gentlemen, pay attention! Sometimes people aren't being kind just for the sake of being kind. They are preying on your vulnerability or naiveté. I still see him from time to time, and I just say a prayer for him and for me. To forgive doesn't mean you forget; it simply means there are no longer any bitter feelings in your heart!

Even though I didn't show it, I was still dealing with hurt from church. Every Sunday I would show up and teach the pre-teens I was responsible for: grades 6-8. Being able to pour into them was very empowering for me. According to Proverbs 11:25 paraphrased, *when we encourage others, we are also encouraged*, and for me, it helped me to continue my healing process.

Our company was one of the many that was attacked by vicious malware and we had to go dark at the beginning of 2020. Can any of you remember life before computers and the internet? We did everything on paper and with carbon copies, which is so inconvenient today. Then the pandemic hit. My state experienced its first confirmed Coronavirus case on January 22, 2020, according to the CDC. At that time, we didn't realize the severity of the virus. Silently killing more people than AIDS, this invisible virus was vicious. Currently, 12,750 people have died in my state alone, and the U.S. has lost 993,000 lives.[10] Most people wore masks and remained socially distant. Despite being a pain, it played a critical role in slowing the spread.

In March it was like the world completely shut down, and the company I work for decided to have employees work remotely to help stop the spread of COVID19. I learned a lot about myself and others during 2020. Many of us relied on being able to congregate and hang out, but now with this invisible virus, we had to be cautious.

It was during this downtime that I came to love myself more. Deep inner reflection has helped me understand who I am as a whole. It has made me more aware of what makes me and I have not allowed situations or people to break me. A few times I was upset regarding friends with whom I have lost contact. But I had to check myself and realize that each of us was dealing with this pandemic differently. It was important to realize that our sisterhood and love for one another was so much stronger than the circumstance we were facing. We needed to lift each other up in prayer continually.

My relationship with my dad grew stronger. He has taught me so much about who he is as a Black man in America. I missed out on so many life lessons because he was gone, but he is around now, so that is what matters. Instead of wasting time and energy on what didn't happen, I have decided to make new memories here and now.

Just before the world shutdown, I was introduced to comedian Flame Monroe on *The Breakfast Club*, which I found mesmerizing. It's no secret that I love comedy, and she was being politically incorrect, and I couldn't stop laughing. So I immediately went and subscribed to all of her social media platforms.

On March 18th Flame started her Instagram daily LIVE videos and thus started our new family of flamettes, vouchettes, and firecrackers. I needed these daily check-ins to stay motivated. One

---

10

particular episode, number 177 on July 16, 2020, Flame had brought on Reverend Porter and First Lady Catrice to speak about current events. One topic that was discussed was a murderous romance. Particularly, who was at fault for this tragedy? After the discussion, Reverend Porter prayed specifically for the young man who murdered a transgender woman in Chicago and for our nation, our world and those of us on the LIVE. His words reminded me of the Love of God. And that love drives hate away. One day, the family of the murdered transwoman may be able to forgive the young man who killed her, and the young man may also be able to forgive himself. Because of God's forgiveness towards me, who am I that I cannot forgive others? In that moment, God restored my faith in the church and brought healing to me. The love of God covered me like a warm blanket, and protected me from me the cold I had been experiencing. I felt at peace. I am so grateful for a God who is always there when I am open and willing to receive Him.

I met with my pastors on Saturday, October 3rd, so we could come to a place of healing and understanding. In that moment, they felt in their hearts that letting me go helped me, but I was extremely hurt. By making this decision, they hoped to alleviate one or more stressors in my life so that I could focus more on what I need to do. People often never reach a place of healing because they can't let go of pride. We often interpret a situation differently than it was intended to be. When that decision was made, it put me in a bad emotional, mental, and spiritual space. We had been so close and now we are so far apart. Eventually I realized that it was all God's doing. While I had been holding on to the rejection personally, God knew I needed to be free for my son's health concerns.

As you read this, I want to encourage you to make time for those who are important to you. Make the decision now to talk to someone if you feel that you have been hurt or wronged in any way. You must also be open to the possibility that your actions may have affected how they felt. Don't wait to contact them. Most people wait for a better moment to do these things when there is no better time than now. Tomorrow isn't guaranteed. As COVID19 has reminded us **ALL, TIME** is not on our side, so take action **NOW!** We must practice forgiveness and let go of past mistakes. Forgiveness doesn't mean that you will no longer think about it; it just means that your heart is no longer hurting because of it. Some people come into your life for a season, and some for a lifetime, but you must not mix the two up.

It's common for us to get down on ourselves when we realize how we have made different choices and decisions, but it's not healthy. Recognize where you were in your journey when you made those decisions. Exactly what pushed you in that direction? At times in my life, I was at a breaking point; I was confused, misunderstood, and yearning for something I didn't have. On more than one occasion, I was seeking something I thought I needed. We all have a life to live, and it's up to us to make the most of it. I am grateful for the lessons I have learned over the years. To God be the glory!

What have I learned? I have learned that I enjoy being loved. My top two love languages in a romantic relationship are quality time and physical touch. You should take the time to find out what your 5 love languages are.[11] I like having adult conversations. When I am alone with myself, I feel content. Over the years I have learned that I am an encourager to a lot of people, but I must work on cheering for myself. As a result of this pandemic, I have had to do a lot of self-encouragement. Despite my flaws, I have learned to love myself. I had to learn how to make peace with my past, focus on my present, and work toward my future. Throughout my life, everything has happened for a reason. Does my story end here? Absolutely Not! As I have breath in my lungs, a fight in my spirit, and my heart is beating, my life journey will continue. I encourage you to live your life to your fullest potential. Our fellow flammette and honorary aunty, TT Janet always says, "Manage your life like your running a Fortune 500 Company!" Don't let fear take control and stop you from what God has for you! Will you make mistakes? Yes, you will. Your job is to learn from the mistakes and keep it pushing forward.

11

You may ask, "Who am I"? I am a Black woman living in America! I am free and I am not alone! I am of a mixed ethnicity but when you see me, you see a Black woman. My African roots come from West Africa with an emphasis on Nigeria! My ancestors have passed on so many gifts and talents to me and I must tap into them. To honor my African heritage and my self-love, I choose to wear my hair in its natural state, straight out of my head. Sometimes I am obnoxious and loud. I may come off as rude when I am being direct, but that is not my intent. In the mornings, I look in the mirror and tell myself that I am beautiful. My daily statements to myself are much more important than what anyone else says to me, and **I LOVE ME! I AM THE GRAND PRIZE!!** I'm the proud mother of four beautiful children who are now fine adults. I enjoy listening to music, particularly gangster rap and 90s R&B. Both of my sons rap and sing. Their solo stage names are Professor J00G and D'reigns and have a group called ShedCr3w. You can find their music on all streaming platforms. I used to write poetry when I was a teenager. In the midst of so much turmoil, that was one of the ways I kept my sanity. Even today, I still have the poems and read them periodically to see how my mind has matured. I love God and I'm saved and sanctified by my Black Jesus. My FAITH has kept me in every sense of the word. Although I love to sing, I can't hold a tune. I love to dance but sometimes can't find the rhythm; I get that from my momma! I enjoy doing home improvements and I am constantly reminded of how far I've come. I love to laugh and crack corny jokes. My favorite hobby is reading! Museums are my passion! In particular, I love learning about history, especially if it involves the history of my people. It was in South Carolina that I got to touch a cotton field while picturing my ancestors and what they had to endure, and that made me appreciate myself more. There was a sense that I belonged here for a greater purpose. My success in life is a gift to my ancestors who fought so hard before me. It brought me back to a time in 2015, when we visited our great aunt Gladys. I always enjoyed hearing her stories. During this particular day, she told me a story about when she was five years old and she couldn't attend school because she had to pick cotton. It would take her all day to pick just two rows of cotton. Unfortunately, she never learned how to read. The field I stood in extended for miles and was very low to the ground. When I think about the back-breaking work my ancestors did, day in and day out, in the rain, snow or scorching sun and they still smiled, I am in awe. Life will never be easy, but try to make the best of it. I discover new things about myself every day. Sometimes I like what I find, sometimes I don't, and in those cases I adjust.

Let me leave you with this: Never stop discovering who you are. As you grow, your world expands. Some of the people and situations you started with will not finish with you. You realize the adventures you loved once no longer make you happy. Don't take life for granted. Every event has a purpose. It is common for us to not understand an incident as it happens, but when we reflect on it, those Ah-ha moments occur. Show love to people in whatever way you can. Doing good for others and it will return to you in unexpected ways. Whenever bad things happen, try to find the lesson as it's always there. Remember that God is love, and love conquers hate. Let us continue to show love to one another, in the hope of a brighter and better future!

Always remember to **LIVE** life to the fullest, **LAUGH** at everything, and **LOVE** unconditionally!

Acknowledgments

First and foremost, I want to thank God; without Him I am nothing. Through it ALL, He has not left me! I am grateful to my ancestors who have guided me.

Thank you personally to my beautiful children; Boogie, Olivia, David, and Sienna for being the best that God has to offer. I thank you for choosing me to be your mom. It wasn't always easy, but we made it! I love you with ALL of me! And to my nieces and nephews, who had the honor of living with us, consider yourselves blessed. Not to mention our dogs Baby Ganja (BG) (RIP), Buster (RIP), Ganja, and Gina – Woof Woof!

To my grandma Geraldine, who has always been my number one. You will always be my angel. I miss you terribly. Likewise, Grandpa Don! To my uncle David and Grandpa Karch, you both rock! Kisses to the sky! My mom Marjorie who loved me the best way she knew how. I miss you so much, Mommy! Thank you to my brother Tyson and sister Celeste for putting up with me during this journey. Thank you to my dad, Larry, who may have shown up a little late, but you are still here, and I love you for that! Dad, I so appreciate our every day conversations. I thank my great Aunt Gladys for sharing her life stories with me.

Let me give a big shout out to my girl, my sister: Eleanor. We go back like four flats on a Cadillac, 36 years and counting, and nothing can separate the love we have for each other, and I am grateful for that.

Thank you also to these key players of my life with whom I have been friends from 4-18 years, Lokelani, Fa'afetai, Tina, Elizabeth, Lesia, Chesna, Milagros, Tracee, Terrance, Reginald, and Misty. For being an ear to hear me and a heart to love me, I am thankful. I am blessed to have each of you in my life.

Thank you so much for showing me how to love all of me, Flame Monroe. You have shown me that I am the GRAND PRIZE! I would also like to thank my newest family members, Mark, Bobbie, Jesse and Jules, who have been incredibly helpful behind the scenes. I love you to the moon and back!

Thank you Dr Conrad Webster for reading my first draft and providing the constructive feedback I needed to move forward. Thank you also to my editor, Cate Perry, who read my manuscript twice and helped make my story come alive.

Additionally, I would like to thank my big sister from the Big Brothers and Sisters Organization. As I looked through old pictures, I was reminded of her. While I can't recall her name, she was a significant part of my life from ages 10 to 12. By taking me to restaurants, she introduced me to different types of international cuisines. With her, I also learned to ski and rode my first boat. I thank God for the role you played in my life. Mentorship is so crucial in young person's life.

Thank you to my Pastors Earl, Andrew, and Maile who spoke life into me and brought out the best in me. You saw things in me that I couldn't even see in myself. There are so many more people that I could mention, but right now I am having a brain freeze. Charge it to my head and not my heart.

Everyone who played a small or big part in my continued journey, I am truly blessed to have crossed paths with you. Be it family, a friend, a stranger, or a foe, you made an impact on my life. Nothing happens by accident. Everything has its time, and mine is now! May you all be blessed and enjoy the journey.

A Tribute to Coach Dye

My sweet king, I still dream about the day we met. I learned so much from you, especially about our culture in that short time. I remember you telling me about your trips to Africa and Dubai and the love the people had for you. When you met Dick Gregory in person, you described him as being awesome. There was a special connection between us. You treated me like a Queen! October 22, 2020 was the last time we were together in the same city. Although we were unable to move beyond our friendship, I am honored to have known and loved you.

On March 20, 2019, we first connected via FB messenger. Both of us were members of the same social group. On July 21, 2019, while you were visiting family in Seattle, we met in person for the first time. We walked and talked for two hours on that day. Over the past two years, I've had a lot of conversations with you. During this two year friendship, we hung out five times together. You were wearing the dashiki I bought you at school on March 8th when you sent me your last picture. You received my birthday gift in the mail on March 12, 2021, and that is when COVID19 secretly attack your body. A rapid test on March 13 came back negative. But you still didn't feel well. On March 17, you texted me to let me know you tested positive. The last time we communicated was March 21, 2021. I discovered how serious things had become on March 30. On April 1, 2021, your birthday, I sent a voice message to your daughter. She let you listen to it when she went returned to your room. I told you, I loved you, and I did it, I finally completed my book. You were the one who helped me play with the word (crisis) in my title and for that I am thankful. The transition took place on April 3, 2021, and you have now joined your ancestors.

You accepted me for everything that I was and loved that the woman I was becoming. I am forever grateful to you for showing me how a man should treat a woman! I am not sure if I will ever meet another like you, but if I do, I would be honored. I admired how you opened doors for me and made sure to be outside when we walked the streets of Charlotte, North Carolina. When I was traveling alone, you always checked on me and offered to call some people you knew for me. We often joked about having our daughters compete in a cook off because both are chefs. When I lost my friend Lourdes to COVID19 in December of 2020, you sent me comfort. Originally, we were going to meet up in Portland during the middle of April, but of course that never happened. You made a significant impact on your community in Pageland, South Carolina, and everyone you touched was blessed to know you. You are still in my heart every day and your presence will be greatly missed.

Thank you for all the video and voice messages you sent to me. I watch and listen to them every now and then.

Rest well, my sweet Reginald!

MEMORIES

Above my family 2021 – Right my family 1999

Above my family 2017 – Right my family 2004

Grandma/Mom/Kids/Grandkids -2011

Mom/Kids/Grandkids - 2005

Me and my siblings – 1979

Me and my siblings - 1982

Me and my siblings - 1981

Me and my siblings – 1983

Mom and Me - 1980

Me and my siblings - 1982

Below- Pregnant w/ Boogie 1994

Below – our family 1985

Our family - 1988

Our family - 1986

Me and my cousin – 1986

Ghetto fun – blanket rolling - 1986

My first car – 1993

Fashion Show - 1986

BGD - 1990

Bottom Mad-Pak 1992

California - 2010

Easter Event - 2010

Great America - 2010

Vision Conference - 2010

Our first Sunday - 2004

Christmas Play 2011

Idaho Trip with Mom – 2004

Birthday party - 2006

Vision conference - 2010

Birthday Party - 2002

Christmas – 2004

Birthday Party - 2003

Mom, Dad and Us – 2008

me/mom – 1975

me/mom - 1976

Me and Grandma – 2010
Right – Black Panther Movie - 2018

Mom and Dad - 2008

Mom and Siblings - 2010

Grandpa Karch and Katsue – 2008

Grandma and Grandpa Soper - 2008

Grandma Jeannette - 1979

Aunt Gladys - 2010

"Long live the rose that grew from concrete when no one else even cared."
Tupac Amaru Shakur

❖

"We're made to grow. You either evolve or disappear."
Tupac Amaru Shakur

FOOTNOTES

1. https://parade.com/1237476/jessicasager/tupac-quotes/
2. https://en.wikipedia.org/wiki/Thug_life
3. https://en.wikipedia.org/wiki/Seattle_Housing_Authority
4. https://en.wikipedia.org/wiki/Namu_My%C5%8Dh%C5%8D_Renge_Ky%C5%8D
5. https://en.wikipedia.org/wiki/Blood_In_Blood_Out#:~:text='Blood%20in%20blood%20out'%20refers,La%20Onda%20in%20the%20film.
6. https://www.hawaii-aloha.com/blog/2011/10/12/how-hawaii-celebrates-babys-first-birthday/
7. https://en.wikipedia.org/wiki/Pseudohypoparathyroidism
8. https://www.blackhistorymonth.org.uk/article/section/bhm-intros/marcus-garvey-famously-wrote-a-people

9. https://www.familysearch.org/search/record/results?count=20&q.anyPlace=MISSISSIPPI&q.givenName=JENNIE%20L&q.surname=STOVALL&f.collectionId=1810731
10. https://covid.cdc.gov/covid-data-tracker/#datatracker-home
11. https://www.5lovelanguages.com/

My Daily Affirmations
I urge you to declare and decree these scriptures over your life every day. Words have power!

I AM courageous!	Deuteronomy 31:6
I AM determined!	James 1:12
I AM victorious!	Romans 8:37
I AM loved!	John 3:16
I AM gifted!	1 Peter 4:10
I AM anointed!	1 John 2:20
I AM blessed!	Matthew 5:3-12
I AM successful!	Proverbs 16:3
I AM healed!	Isaiah 53:5; Psalm 147:3
I AM beautiful!	Psalm 139:13-14
I AM whole!	Genesis 2:7
I AM confident!	Isaiah 32:17
I AM strong!	Isaiah 41:10
I AM forgiving!	Matthew 6:14
I AM not afraid!	2 Timothy 1:7
I AM generous!	Luke 6:38
I AM grateful!	1 Thessalonians 5:16-18
I AM able!	Philippians 4:13
I AM favored!	Psalm 84:11
I AM God's masterpiece!	Ephesians 2:10

I AM A BLACK WOMAN EMPOWERED!!

MORE FROM THE AUTHOR

If you would like to invite Cassandra to speak at your event or appear on your podcast/YouTube channel, you can contact her via email:
cassiekarch@gmail.com

Hashtag **#IdentityCrySis** and please tag me to show support for my work!
Instagram @cassiekarch   Twitter @cassiekarch

Made in the USA
Middletown, DE
12 May 2022

65652213R00076